T0276336

America's Fortress

FLORIDA HISTORY AND CULTURE

UNIVERSITY PRESS OF FLORIDA

Florida A&M University, Tallahassee
Florida Atlantic University, Boca Raton
Florida Gulf Coast University, Ft. Myers
Florida International University, Miami
Florida State University, Tallahassee
New College of Florida, Sarasota
University of Central Florida, Orlando
University of Florida, Gainesville
University of North Florida, Jacksonville
University of South Florida, Tampa
University of West Florida, Pensacola

A History of Fort Jefferson, Dry Tortugas, Florida

Thomas Reid

University Press of Florida
Gainesville · Tallahassee · Tampa · Boca Raton
Pensacola · Orlando · Miami · Jacksonville · Ft. Myers · Sarasota

First cloth printing, 2006
First paperback printing, 2022

27 26 25 24 23 22   6 5 4 3 2 1

A record of cataloging-in-publication data is available from the
Library of Congress.

ISBN 978-0-8130-3019-7 (CLOTH) | ISBN 978-0-8130-8004-8 (PBK.)

The University Press of Florida is the scholarly publishing agency
for the State University System of Florida, comprising Florida
A&M University, Florida Atlantic University, Florida Gulf Coast
University, Florida International University, Florida State University,
New College of Florida, University of Central Florida, University of
Florida, University of North Florida, University of South Florida,
and University of West Florida.

University Press of Florida
2046 NE Waldo Road
Suite 2100
Gainesville, FL 32609
http://upress.ufl.edu

This work is dedicated to the Rangers of the National Park Service—
preserving and making America's history available
and understandable to all generations.

CONTENTS

FOREWORD

America's Fortress is the latest volume in a series devoted to the study of Florida history and culture. During the past half century, the burgeoning growth and increased national and international visibility of Florida have sparked a great deal of popular interest in the state's past, present, and future. As the favorite destination of hordes of tourists and as the new home for millions of retirees, immigrants, and transplants, modern Florida has become a demographic, political, and cultural bellwether.

A state of vast distances and tumultuous change, Florida needs more citizens who care about the welfare of this special place and its people. We hope this series helps newcomers and old timers appreciate and understand Florida. The University Press of Florida established the Florida History and Culture Series in an effort to provide an accessible and attractive format for the publication of works related to the Sunshine State.

As coeditors of the series, we are deeply committed to the creation of an eclectic but carefully crafted set of books that will provide the field of Florida studies with a fresh focus and encourage Florida researchers and writers to consider the broader implications and context of their work. The series includes monographs, memoirs, anthologies, and travelogues. And, while the series features books of historical interest, we encourage authors researching Florida's environment, politics, and popular or material culture to submit their manuscripts as well. We want each book to retain a distinct personality and voice, but at the same time we hope to foster a sense of community and collaboration among Florida scholars.

In *America's Fortress: A History of Fort Jefferson, Dry Tortugas, Florida,* Thomas Reid weaves a fascinating account of a place few Floridians—and even fewer Americans—have encountered. Fort Jefferson towers over the Dry Tortugas, the farthermost place in America's southernmost state. For well over a century, military technology has made Fort Jefferson an isolated relic amid coral reefs and bird-inhabited islands, but Reid's research uncovers an extraordinary array of characters and events that make *America's Fortress* a compelling read.

Reid begins his narrative with a simple but powerful sentence: "A history of Fort Jefferson is much more than the story of the most heavily armed coastal defense fort ever built by the United States." Indeed! Since it was named "Las Tortugas" (The Turtles—from the pre-millennia loggerheads and green turtles that returned each year) by Juan Ponce de León in 1513, few places have attracted such an odd collection of characters and served as such a place of sheer intrigue and utter boredom.

From a modest lighthouse and cottage in 1825, Fort Jefferson became the "American Gibraltar," a truly remarkable fortress that swallowed federal dollars and doomed countless sailors and soldiers, guards and prisoners to a desolate fate. The parade of historical characters is simply fascinating: John J. Audubon, the famed painter of American birds; Brigadier General Joseph Gilbert Totten, a brilliant military engineer; hundreds of slaves who faithfully—and sometimes not so faithfully—constructed powder magazines and massive masonry walls and towers; New York Zouaves with their colorful uniforms and names; troops of the 90th New York, who melted under the merciless summer sun and outbreaks of yellow fever; the Second Regiment U.S. Colored Troops; thousands of hapless Union prisoners who endured courts-martial, weevil-infested bread, scurvy, and hurricanes; Dr. Samuel Mudd, the star-crossed physician who assisted John Wilkes Booth; and naturalists who came to appreciate the archipelago for its stunning bird and marine life. Since 1935, Fort Jefferson has been protected as the Dry Tortugas National Park. What a history!

Raymond Arsenault and Gary R. Mormino
Series Editors

Introduction

A history of Fort Jefferson is much more than the story of the most heavily armed coastal defense fort ever built by the United States. It is also the tale of a remarkably beautiful place, the islands known as the Dry Tortugas, virtually unchanged in the five hundred years since their discovery. Located at the western extreme of the Florida Keys, these small white coral and sand islets are the destination every spring of thousands of breeding sea birds and the huge sea turtles of the Gulf of Mexico and the Atlantic. The surrounding waters are filled with a remarkable variety of fish, corals, and other marine organisms. John J. Audubon, naturalist and writer, described much of the United States in the early 1800s prior to its development. He believed the Tortugas to be a fascinating environment. First set aside as a national monument by President Franklin Roosevelt in 1935, the islands are now protected as the Dry Tortugas National Park.

A small lighthouse and cottage were built on one of the larger keys in 1825. Construction on the fort known in several documents as the "American Gibraltar" began in 1846 and went on for nearly thirty years before the project was abandoned while still incomplete. For nearly twenty years Fort Jefferson was a favored project of Brigadier General Joseph Gilbert Totten, the chief of Army Engineers. Under his leadership that branch of service was entrusted not only with fortifications but also with the building of the national Capitol building, the Washington Aqueduct, and other major public works in that city. Totten's influence in Congress was so strong that despite the fact that more powerful rifled naval guns made masonry forts designed like the one in the Dry Tortugas obsolete, funding for the project actually increased following the outbreak of the American Civil War and was continued for ten years after his death in April 1864. Fort Jefferson was a federal program that simply would not die. Each time its strategic or tactical importance seemed lost, a new justification was concocted. It was at various times the strategic center of U.S. naval forces in the Gulf of Mexico, a major naval supply depot and coaling station, a key to the Union effort to blockade the Confederacy, a military detention center, and a maximum security prison for federal civilian prisoners.

Amid a changeless procession of hurricanes, tropical heat, epidemic disease, and natural cycles totally foreign to the majority of its workmen, engineers, soldiers, and convicts, construction at Fort Jefferson continued. In the beginning slaves provided the majority of unskilled labor. When slavery ceased to exist the War Department simply substituted military personnel convicted by courts-martial and sentenced to hard labor. In modern terms, the challenge was similar to building on another planet; every brick, every plank, every stone, and every worker was shipped in from some distant point. Records in the National Archives and elsewhere document the expenses each year in detail. The record of the cost in terms of human life is more scattered and fragmentary. It is often impossible to correlate numbers with names. Even the nearby sandy keys that served as the post's burial ground have been swept away and reformed as a result of a century of tropical storms, giving truth to the phrase "until the sea gives up its dead."

Fort Jefferson was also the scene of great self-sacrifice and drama during the difficult days of the Civil War and beyond. It became the focus of intense national interest when it was chosen as the site for the incarceration of Dr. Samuel Mudd and the other survivors of the conspiracy to murder President Lincoln. Stories of bravery and selfless service during the frequent outbreaks of yellow fever are common. Although remote and isolated, like any small city it was home to scoundrels and saints and, despite every logical reason to suspect dark and negative outcomes, seems to have balanced good and evil with as much success as any other human community. Even those who constantly complained of the confinement write of the beauty of the sunsets and the surrounding panorama of nature. Although soldiers would be loath to admit it, the peace and orderly routines of a garrison remote from any conflict or battlefield had to lend a feeling of security that others could only hope for. It was a strange, otherworldly environment, partly natural and partly man-made. It was a castle of vast walls and towers rising from the mists of a blue-green tropical sea, defying all logic and stereotype.

The construction of Fort Jefferson began during the height of a period of coastal defense strategy known as the Third System (1816–67). The earlier First System forts dating from the administrations of Washington through Jefferson (1794–1807) were primarily earthworks, sometimes reinforced with wood or masonry. Often too close to the cities they were designed to protect, these works were soon neglected and were rendered indefensible. As tensions with Europe heightened a new Second System of defense was funded by Congress in late 1807. Early construction again depended on simple earthworks but progressed to solid masonry as the War of 1812 with Great Britain approached. Following that war a new defensive strategy would emerge, enabled in part by a generation of engineers trained by the United States Military Academy at West Point.[1]

The burning of the Capitol by the British and the successful defense of Baltimore by Fort McHenry reinforced President James Madison's belief that effective coastal defense was crucial to the nation's welfare. Both Madison and Secretary of State James Monroe were persuaded that expert assistance was needed to ensure the best possible outcome. Upon the recommendation of the Marquis de Lafayette, Congress approved the employment of Simon Bernard, Napoleon's former aide-de-camp and chief of artillery, with the salary equivalent of a brigadier general of engineers. President Madison's belief that Congress would more readily support projects recommended by a recognized expert over the plans of our own military proved correct.[2]

The Fortifications Board was chartered in 1816 and included Bernard, Chief of Engineers Brigadier General Joseph Gardner Swift, Brigadier General William McRee, and engineer Brevet Lieutenant Colonel Joseph Gilbert Totten. The tension caused by being forced to work with a foreigner as an equal led to Swift and McRee's resignation from the army in 1818. Following its preliminary report to Congress that same year, the board consisted of Bernard, Totten, and Captain J. D. Elliot of the U.S. Navy. Work toward a final report progressed and was completed in 1821.

The report that emerged was the first careful analysis of America's defensive needs as well as a strategic plan to meet those requirements. The plan included a prioritized listing of the locations and strength of fortifications, defined the role and support required by the navy, defined the requirements for transportation infrastructure, and outlined the missions of the regular army and the militia. Recognizing that Congress opposed increasing the size of the professional army, the plan envisioned defensive fortifications with small garrisons that could withstand enemy attack for two to three weeks until reinforcements could be called up from local militias. Emanuel Lewis accurately summarized matters: "This bias toward forms of defense that require relatively few men even in war, and practically none in peacetime, was undoubtedly a major factor underlying the predisposition toward seacoast fortifications." For the first time the United States would have a clearly defined and unified defense strategy that fully integrated both major branches of the military.[3]

Simon Bernard continued serving on the Fortifications Board until his return to France in 1830. Leaving the actual construction of the Third System to the U.S. Army Corps of Engineers, in his later years he concentrated on "internal improvements," such as roads and canals necessary for the rapid movement of troops and supplies. This focus on federal infrastructure was not supported by the new administration of Andrew Jackson. The withdrawal of congressional backing for his projects and a favorable change of government in France made Bernard's decision to resign an easy one. His departure left Joseph Totten as the chair of the Fortifications Board. By 1838 Totten became chief of engineers as well, positions he held until his death in 1864.[4]

When Totten assumed duties as chief of engineers in 1838 one of his greatest strengths was his ability to usher his projects through the Congress. Like his predecessor Charles Gratiot, Totten inspired the trust of the legislators by maintaining detailed and highly accurate financial accounts on each construction project. His success was also due to his sensitivity to the changing political environment in which he was required to justify priorities and purposes of each of the public works entrusted to his department. Totten's success often resulted from his ability to tailor his priorities to the political trends that dominated the nation while retaining the appearance of strict professional neutrality.

Recent research by Mark Andrew Smith of the University of Alabama indicated that although debate in Congress concerning the level of funding and construction priorities often became intense, there was no serious or systematic questioning during the antebellum era of the fundamental assumptions of the national defense strategy embodied in the Third System. Smith insightfully points out that wide variations in funding have more to do with the national economy and the internal workings of the Congress than with any doubt about the engineers' ability to define a successful policy for national defense.[5]

By 1838 the political scene was dominated by the new Democratic Party and the movement known as "Young America." As of October 1837 the movement had a focal point in the new *United States Magazine and Democratic Review*. Edited by the highly nationalistic New Yorker John L. O'Sullivan, the periodical boasted Andrew Jackson as its first subscriber. Like President Jackson, the *Democratic Review* opposed the dominance of an economic elite and promoted greater participation in the political process. True to its Jeffersonian principles, the motto on the title page was "The best government is that which governs least." The magazine attracted such literary contributors as Nathaniel Hawthorne and Herman Melville and generally supported reform measures while avoiding the sectional controversy embodied by abolitionism.[6]

Sectional tensions account in part for O'Sullivan's support of increased American expansionism embodied in his belief in America's "Manifest Destiny." In the summer of 1845 he echoed the feeling of many Americans anxious to see the incorporation of the Oregon territory and the Republic of Texas into the United States. He stated that "the fulfillment of our manifest destiny [is] to overspread the continent allotted by Providence for the free development of our yearly multiplying millions." Although O'Sullivan's statements seem a justification for President Polk's later aggressive military actions in Texas that led to the outbreak of the Mexican War, that was probably not his intent. He believed that democratic ideas and institutions would sweep the continent, not American military forces. Biographer Robert Sampson stated that O'Sullivan "simply crafted the 'perfect expression' for an 'enthusiastic belief in American democracy and in the mission of the United States to carry it throughout the North American continent.'"[7]

Chief of Engineers Totten's priorities were very much in keeping with the nation's expansionist attitude as expressed by President James K. Polk's determination to annex Texas and purchase Mexico's northwestern territory. In July 1845 Florida, admitted as a state in March, deeded its strategic offshore islands to the federal government. That action cleared the path for a broadened and updated justification for Third System forts at Key West and the Dry Tortugas. Totten's proposed construction of what became Fort Taylor and Fort Jefferson represented an expression of both the traditional role of defense and the projection of the new American nationalism into the Gulf of Mexico. This dual approach of protection and projection probably assured congressional support as well as that of a Polk administration determined to be credited with the realization of Manifest Destiny.[8]

The proposed scale of Fort Jefferson, 450 guns and a garrison of 1,500, cannot be justified in purely defensive terms. In area it is the third largest of all the installations of the Third System. Its three tiers of 150 guns each, however, are disproportionate for the defense of a remote but strategic point controlling the Straits of Florida. The chief of engineers was meticulous in his calculations. The design of the fort on Garden Key does not reflect a plan that envisioned a brief defense followed by reinforcement by militia. In modern military terms it is a platform designed to project American military power toward Cuba or Central America. Its intimidating size and armament could easily have served as a protected anchorage for a large fleet as well as supplying vast quantities of naval stores and coal for a new generation of steam-powered gunboats. In his November 1, 1851, report to Congress on fortifications, Totten countered any contention that steam batteries (gunboats) could replace forts saying, that batteries "were a valuable supplement to the forts but were useless without them."[9]

Construction at Garden Key began in December 1846. Northern Mexico had fallen, and Joseph Totten was about to embark with General Winfield Scott's invasion force as Scott's chief of engineers. Totten would later be promoted to brevet brigadier general after the successful siege of Vera Cruz. The annexation of the Oregon territory had been ratified by the Senate on June 15, 1846. The Treaty of Guadalupe Hidalgo that ended the Mexican War was signed on February 2, 1848. That treaty transferred much of the West to the United States and established the Rio Grande as the southern border of Texas. O'Sullivan's belief in a national Manifest Destiny seemed to have been secured, but not through the persuasion and attractions of democracy. Nor did its realization have the palliative effect on sectional strife between North and South that had been predicted.[10]

The two decades preceding the American Civil War were a period of turmoil when increasing sectional tension defined domestic politics. In terms of the key leadership positions of the army, however, it was a time of relative stability. General-in-Chief Winfield Scott became the senior army officer in 1841 and retained that distinction until after the outbreak of war in 1861. Although Scott was not a graduate of the U.S. Military Academy, his personal conservatism and firm grounding in European military traditions made him a supporter of a small, well-educated, and professional officer corps. In terms of political influence, however, Scott's ability to promote an army agenda in Congress was limited. President James K. Polk perceived successful commanders like Scott as potential political threats. General Scott's unsuccessful campaign for the presidency in 1852 as a Whig also cost him the reputation for professionalism and political neutrality so necessary to retaining the goodwill of Congress. The stormy relationship between Scott and President Franklin Pierce's secretary of war, Jefferson Davis, further marginalized him in terms of congressional influence.[11]

The army's most powerful and politically active branch was headed by Chief of Engineers Joseph G. Totten from 1838 until his death in April 1864. Throughout those years he was active promoting the interests of the army in Congress, at the same time remaining scrupulously nonpartisan. Totten was in fact the leader of a group of officers lobbying for the programs of the U.S. Army Corps of Engineers. Among the duties of chief engineer was the supervision of the U.S. Military Academy at West Point. Totten was one of the institution's first graduates; he completed his studies and was commissioned in 1805. Political pressures on the army during the period came on three different fronts, all of which took the form of threatened funding cuts by Congress.[12]

Controversies concerning the funding of seacoast fortifications were often divisive. Representatives of the younger western states portrayed the program as "a worthless pork-barrel scheme to spend money in the coastal states." Others questioned the continued need and military utility of such forts in the emerging age of steam-powered ironclad gun ships. Totten and other senior officers in Washington maintained close ties in Congress to counter such trends. Junior officers supervising construction were strongly encouraged to build political support for projects in their areas. This often extended, as in the case of Fort Jefferson, to hiring workmen and purchasing materials in local markets. Officers were also expected to write articles for regional and national publications that would highlight the crucial position that coastal fortifications played in the nation's military strategy. The most serious threat to the program's funding came in 1851 when the House of Representatives effectively killed the Fortifications Bill for fiscal year 1852. After intense lobbying by the engineers and their supporters in Congress funding was restored the next year.[13]

Another figure among senior engineer officers was Richard Delafield, who graduated first in the West Point class of 1818. A fervent believer in coastal defenses, he served as superintendent of the Military Academy from 1838 to 1845 and again from 1856 to 1861. In 1855 he organized the Delafield Commission and was sent by Secretary of War Jefferson Davis to evaluate and observe military developments in Europe as well as to report on the ongoing Siege of Sevastopol and the Crimean War. The reports of the commission were probably crucial in cementing congressional support for funding ongoing construction of seacoast forts during the final four years of the antebellum era.[14]

A second perennial issue that troubled the Corps of Engineers was the assault on the Military Academy as an "aristocratic institution" embodying values incompatible with those of a democracy. Totten vigorously defended the need for a technical military education and a professional officer corps. In 1842 he directed the superintendent of West Point to collect data quietly on the family background of new cadets, information that was later used successfully by the War Department to reassure Congress of the broad democratic nature of admissions. Notwithstanding any demographics supporting the cadets' egalitarian origins, the fact remained that the best graduates were invariably offered engineer commissions. If not a military aristocracy, that branch certainly formed an elite group within the army.[15]

The structure and strength of the regular army authorized by Congress was a third political issue that had an impact on the army and the Corps of Engineers. The activation of both regular and volunteer units for the Mexican War was the occasion for the commissioning of citizens by the president, often as a reward for political support. In the process officers with regular commissions and graduates of the U.S. Military Academy were often denied promotion into positions in the new units. Although such favoritism caused a great deal of dissent among infantry and artillery officers, the technical branches such as engineers were largely insulated. In terms of promotion, technical branch officers were guaranteed promotion to captain after fourteen years' service without respect to vacancies. This was due primarily to legislation carefully guided through Congress by Joseph Totten in 1852.[16]

One of the stranger uses of Fort Jefferson during the course of the Civil War was its designation as a federal prison, primarily for Union soldiers convicted by court martial. This was not based on any coherent plan by the War Department but was mainly driven by expediency. Recruiting by volunteer regiments, the growth of wartime industries, and the draft quickly absorbed the workforce that had earlier been contracted for skilled and unskilled labor in the Tortugas. These workers were, in theory, replaced by soldier convicts. In reality engineer supervisors found that due to scurvy, tropical fevers, and disability the number of prisoners actually capable of construction duty seldom exceeded one-fifth of the population. Nearly twenty-four hundred convicts passed through the gates of Fort Jefferson between 1861 and 1874. The peak came as the war drew to a close in the fall of 1864, when the number incarcerated neared nine hundred. Quartered in boarded-in casemates, few prisoners could actually be effectively secured and guarded.

The offenders' crimes ranged from petty theft and political dissent against the Lincoln administration to rape, robbery, and murder. As actual prisons and expedient facilities like Fort Delaware and Fort Monroe in the North were filled, Fort Jefferson received the overflow as well as convicted Confederate blockade runners and later opponents of military Reconstruction in the South. The near total isolation of the Tortugas and the virtual impossibility of escape, along with severe punishments, were among the factors that allowed the garrison to maintain relative control of more unruly elements. Duties demanded by the need to supervise the prison population were frequent causes for complaints in the letters and diaries of both officers and enlisted soldiers.

During the nineteenth century the terms *fort* and *fortress* were often used indiscriminately despite the fact that the latter implies a defensive structure surrounding a town. During the years of its most intensive occupation Fort Jefferson did in fact become a fortress surrounding a lively village occupied by civilian workmen, slaves, families, professionals, soldiers, fishermen, and convicts. For a time its uniquely national character and location truly made it America's fortress.

Defender of a Young America

1824–1859

Responding to a request from the U.S. Senate, the Navy Commissioners' Office addressed inquiries regarding the possible location of naval depots and fortifications in Florida. In summarizing the findings of the commission, John Rodgers wrote to the secretary of the navy on April 15, 1824. "It is recommended that competent officers of the Engineers be directed to ascertain the probable expense of erecting such fortifications as will render Thompson's Island [Key West], or the Dry Tortugas, a secure anchorage for vessels in time of war. Either of these places have a sufficient depth of water for vessels of the largest class; and if they can be rendered secure from attack, will form highly valuable positions, in conjunction with a depot at Pensacola, for the protection of our commerce, passing to and from the Mississippi, and other ports in the Gulf of Mexico."[1]

One observer who was decidedly unimpressed with the Tortugas as the potential site of a naval depot was Commodore David Porter, who had visited the keys in December 1824 and January 1825. Porter wrote: "The islands consist of small sand Islands a little above the surface of the Ocean, on some of which is some low shrubbery, but all are liable to changes from gales of wind. Their insulated situation, and distance from the continent renders blockade easy; they have a good inner harbor for small craft and a tolerable outer one for ships of war; but they have no fresh water, and furnish scarcely land enough to place a fortification and it is doubtful if they have solidity enough to bear one."[2] Later subsidence of the walls of Fort Jefferson indicated that Porter's estimate of the load-bearing abilities of the Tortugas was quite accurate.

Among the first to suggest that the islands of the Dry Tortugas were a logical "anchor" for a chain of forts defending the coast of the United States from Maine to the mouth of the Mississippi was Lieutenant Josiah Tattnall. In 1829 Tattnall sailed aboard the U.S. sloop *Florida* and completed a survey of the keys. His observations were later included in the proceedings of Congress. "A naval force, designed to control the navigation of the Gulf, could desire no better position than . . . the Tortugas. . . . And there can be no doubt that an adversary, in possession of large naval means, would, with great advantage, make these harbors his habitual resort. [Our occupation would] transfer to our own squadron, even should it be inferior, these most valuable positions; and it would afford a point of refuge to our navy and to our commerce at the very spot where it would be most necessary and useful."[3] Memories of British naval assaults against ports of the United States during the War of 1812 were still quite fresh, and the successful defense of Baltimore by Fort McHenry had become a symbol of national pride. Tattnall's highly favorable report was forwarded by Secretary of the Navy John Branch to President Andrew Jackson on March 25, 1830, but the navy soon lost interest in the Tortugas as work progressed on the new base established at Pensacola, Florida.[4]

The small cluster of barren islands later christened Las Tortugas was first seen by the Spanish explorer Juan Ponce de León on the summer solstice, June 21, 1513.[5] On that longest day of the year, the sun's blinding glare would have reflected from the white coral sand. The larger islands were covered with low brush and a few mangroves and other small trees, twisted and stunted by the prevailing winds. Despite the uninviting look of the featureless bits of land, the waters teemed with marine life. The clear shallows revealed walls and floors of coral that harbored brilliantly colored fish, eels, and large sharks. The three small ships lay at anchor in the bay, where they made repairs and spent time ashore. The combination of heat and humidity would have been nearly intolerable. Almost three hundred and fifty years later, one soldier stationed there remarked, "if there is a Hell . . . I don't believe it is much hotter then Tortugas."[6]

As night fell the Spaniards observed processions of huge turtles emerge from the sea and slowly crawl inland to scoop depressions in the sand to lay and bury their eggs. The turtles made a significant contribution to the mariners' supply of meat. "On Tuesday the 21st, they reached the rocky islets, which they named *Las Tortugas*, because in one short time in the night they took, in one of these islands, one hundred and sixty tortoises, and might have taken more if they had wanted them. They took also fourteen seals, and there were killed many pelicans and other birds."[7] June was the height of the season when thousands of terns and other sea birds occupied nearly every square foot of sand in a noisy ritual of nesting and raising their young. By the end of June 1513 the fleet departed, taking with them no impressions likely to tempt other Europeans to repeat their visit, except perhaps for meat. Later, the position of the islands was recognized as a sheltered anchorage on the primary sea lane leading from the Gulf of Mexico through the Straits of Florida to the open Atlantic Ocean. For that reason it was a favored location for privateers lying in wait for the Spanish treasure ships loaded with bullion from the mines of Mexico and Peru.

The first permanent settlement on the Tortugas came six years after the United States acquired Florida as a result of negotiations between Secretary of State John Q. Adams and the Spanish minister Luis de Onis in 1819. A lighthouse was constructed on Bush Key, later known as Garden Key, in April 1826, to warn ships away from the dangerous shoals and reefs surrounding the most westerly of the Florida Keys.[8] The Adams-Onis treaty and the purchase of Florida had several important consequences, one of which was the creation of a continuous national coastline from Maine to the port city of New Orleans. The defense of that coastline would emerge as a strategic goal of the United States second only to the fortification of the western frontier.

The first evidence of action to plan construction on what was to be the nation's most heavily armed coastal defense fort dates from November 1844, when Captain John G. Barnard of the Corps of Engineers made a detailed reconnaissance of Key West and the Tortugas. He concluded that if the $50,000 appropriated by Congress that year had to be committed immediately, it should be expended on Key West, since the requirement for fortification of the Tortugas would be far more complex and extensive.[9]

Reports described Garden Key as a roughly oval island slightly less than a thousand feet in length. At no point did Garden Key exceed three feet above sea level. The limited foliage consisted of mangroves, cactus, buttonwood trees, and trailing vines. A brackish, stagnant pond had earlier marked the island's center but had been filled in as a result of complaints by the lighthouse keeper that it was "malodorous" and bred mosquitoes.[10]

Following the inauguration of President James K. Polk on March 4, 1845, events rapidly fell in step with the drumbeat of expansion and the calls for the nation to realize its Manifest Destiny. The Territory of Florida had gained statehood on March 3, 1845, and its legislature yielded strategic offshore lands to the federal government in July. The Dry Tortugas became a national military reservation by executive order on September 17, 1845.[11] The next month voters in Texas supported annexation and ratified a new constitution, which quickly gained approval in Congress. President Polk signed the act granting Texas statehood on December 29, 1845. Earlier, Polk had sent Senator John Slidell of Louisiana to Mexico to negotiate a diplomatic solution to questions concerning the borders of Texas as well as to offer to purchase Mexican territories in the West. By March 1846 it became clear that Slidell's mission was a failure. Polk then ordered U.S. forces in Texas commanded by General Zachary Taylor to cross the Nueces River into disputed territory and take up positions on the Rio Grande, the action that triggered the Mexican War.

On November 6, 1845, one year after Barnard's exploratory visit to the Tortugas, Congress received an update from the army. "We learn from the report of Colonel Abert, that the Corps of Topographical Engineers 'consists of forty-three officers, several of whom are brevet second lieutenants.' Of this small force, there were, at the date of the report . . . six on the survey of the Dry Tortugas, and the reefs of Florida."[12] The squad of engineers found the inhabitants of Garden Key to be the lighthouse keeper, John Thompson, his family, and a shifting collection of fishermen and unsavory salvage crews known as "wreckers." The wreckers' livelihood depended on the frequent groundings and shipwrecks caused by the keys' numerous reefs and shoals. The engineers surveyed and mapped the islands and examined borings of the coral sand subsoil in order to determine its load-bearing strength. The only permanent structure other than the lighthouse was a small cottage with a wide veranda shaded by coconut palms and surrounded by black and red mangrove trees. The island and picturesque cottage had been used by author James Fenimore Cooper as the setting for his novel *Jack Tiers*.[13]

Legends suggest that the Dry Tortugas had been a frequent destination of pirates and buccaneers of the West Indies for several hundred years. Captain Benner, a later lighthouse keeper, spent his leisure time searching for treasure and pirate antiquities. He reportedly recovered more than a thousand dollars in silver from nearby East Key as well as brass and iron cannon barrels from the reefs.[14] In practical terms, it would be difficult to draw any clear line between the pirates and the transient population of wreckers who made the Tortugas their occasional base of operations. Subsequent commanders of Fort Jefferson found the wreckers troublesome in that they often frequented ports such as Havana, where yellow fever was endemic, and defied all efforts at quarantine. The transient boatmen also carried on a trade in illicit liquor, which later often found its way to construction workers.

Congress declared war on Mexico on May 13, 1846. By September, General Zachary Taylor had occupied Monterrey and General Winfield Scott's larger army was preparing to sail into the Gulf of Mexico. Work on the fortress on Garden Key began in December 1846 under the supervision of Second Lieutenant Horatio Gouverneur Wright, an engineer and 1841 U.S. Military Academy graduate.[15] The mission fell to Wright when the more senior Captain William Fraser was diverted from the task by the chief of engineers in July 1846 to join the invasion force of Brigadier General John Wool then being staged at San Antonio, Texas.[16] By November 1846 all plans for the fort's structures had been completed. They were approved by Secretary of War William Marcy the same month.[17]

The plans for the fort, drawn by engineer Lieutenant Montgomery Meigs based on a design by Joseph Totten, called for a hexagon-shaped outline with two sides shortened to conform to the shape of Garden Key (fig. 1). The two short walls, or curtains, measured 325 feet and the remaining four walls 477 feet, enclosing a parade or open space of nearly thirteen acres or 63,000 square yards. Each of two tiers of gunrooms or casemates would accommodate 150 cannons, shielded by masonry walls between five and eight feet thick. An additional 150 guns could be mounted on top of the structure, nearly fifty feet above the parade. At each corner of the fort there was to be a bastion containing gunrooms, magazines, and a circular granite staircase. Six detached larger magazines, a headquarters, hospital, and three large barracks and officer quarters would be located on the parade. An early cost estimate for completion was $1.2 million.[18]

Two of the civilian contractors who arrived with Wright aboard the engineer supply schooner *Activa* were Jeremiah Peabody, a carpenter, and George Phillips, a master mason. The schooner had sailed from New York on December 1, 1846, and arrived on December 15. The ship was manned by the captain and a crew of five. Once ashore, Peabody supervised the construction of a rough shelter while Wright and Phillips staked out locations for workers' quarters, the construction office, and sheds for materials. A total of nine civilian workers was reported assigned to the project in November, and ten were present on Garden Key in December.[19] The additional worker listed in December may indicate that Wright hired the lighthouse keeper's slave.

One of Lieutenant Wright's concerns was possible damage done to the site by a major hurricane in early October. The lighthouse keeper reported that on October 11–12, "the surf swept over the entire key except for a small sand ridge on the western end. One of the wharves was wrecked, several small buildings were flattened and all the vessels in the harbor were damaged." Once he arrived at Garden Key, Wright did a thorough survey of

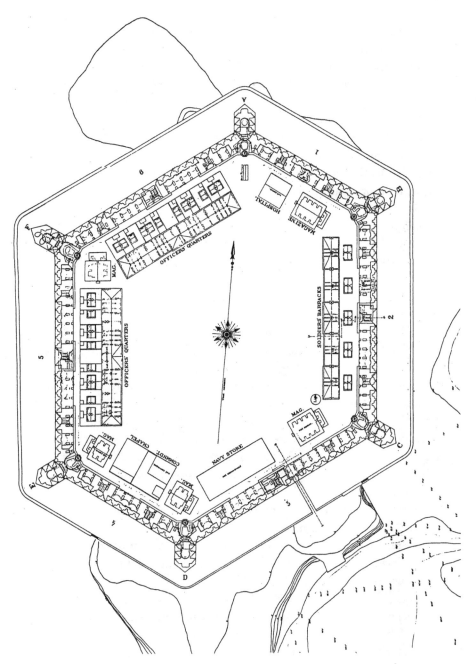

Figure 1. Plan for the completion of Fort Jefferson as approved by the Fortifications Board in 1877. Courtesy National Archives, Records Group 77 (Chief of Engineers), Drawer 74, Sheet 1.

the storm damage. He found that the shape of the island had been altered by huge quantities of sand being shifted from the northern shore to the south. In the inner harbor, areas formerly seven or eight feet deep had been entirely filled with sand and coral debris. After the new survey, Wright was provided with updated plans for the foundations and walls.[20]

The Engineer Department awarded a contract for the buildings to be pre-fabricated and erected by the firm of Parker and Norton within sixty days. But the company went bankrupt and the contract had to be announced a second time. The successful bidder, Andrew B. Vennard, was unable to comply with the original schedule. Workers and materials arrived in the summer of 1847 and were further delayed by the primitive working conditions. By September 7 they had completed a carpenter shop, a dining facility with kitchen, a blacksmith shop, a building to store lime for mortar, and a workers' barracks. The remaining three temporary structures were finished that fall after the end of the fiscal year on September 30 and were not included in the 1847 annual report.[21] There was later agreement that unacclimated white workers accomplished about half as much in the tropical heat as they would have in a temperate environment. It was for that reason that Florida historian Albert Manucy concluded: "Slaves were the backbone of the labor gang, sweating in the broiling sun, sloshing in the tepid water, digging the foundations for the ponderous walls, dumping barrow after barrow of mortar into the forms."[22] The engineers hired the slaves from their owners at Key West as well as occasionally from lighthouse keeper John Thompson.

Both the white contract labor and additional slaves arrived at Garden Key in the summer of 1847. As the heat grew more oppressive, six of the Key West slaves and one belonging to Thompson stole a schooner anchored in the inner harbor and sailed out into the Gulf, perhaps hoping to reach the Florida Everglades and the Seminole Indians, always receptive to runaway slaves. The following morning Lieutenant Wright and John Thompson soon discovered that a telescope, clothing, and a water cask were also missing. The errant slaves were apprehended by a passing ship and eventually returned to their owners at Key West, who quickly restored most of them to the questionable comforts of Garden Key. The slave owners were being paid twenty dollars per slave per month and were understandably anxious to keep them on the job. The two ringleaders of the escape were identified as Jerry Mason and Jack English and remained in Key West.[23]

Wright reported to the chief of engineers that measures were in place to reduce the likelihood of another such incident. "To prevent another attempt on the part of the Negroes to escape and to guard against anything like an insurrection I have deemed it advisable to establish a night watch and have therefore employed Captain Thompson the Light Keeper for that service at $1.00 per night." He pointed out that the "character and dispositions" of the labor force were impossible to determine in advance and that these precautions would also have the effect of reassuring slave owners that their property was secure and making it likely that the primary source of labor would be readily available in Key West.[24]

In late 1850 the fort was officially christened Fort Jefferson by the War Department in honor of the late president.[25] About the same time, long-time Garden Key lighthouse keeper Captain John Thompson retired and was replaced by thirty-three-year-old Benjamin H. Kerr, who continued in the position until the summer of 1858. By 1856 Fort Jefferson appeared in a magazine article that listed specifications including facilities for 298 guns and a required wartime garrison of 1,500 soldiers. The amount so far expended was stated as $210,138, and the projected amount for completion was $989,862. This listing is one of a few early references that accurately describe the post as occupying Garden Key in the Tortugas, Florida.[26] The years 1850 through 1854 saw annual construction spending of appropriations by Congress vary from a low of $5,100 in 1852 to a high of $50,000 in 1854. The average was slightly less than $30,000. Had spending continued at that rate, the completion of the work would have dragged on for over thirty more years.[27]

The year 1855, however, witnessed a dramatic change in spending priorities. The War Department allocated nearly $164,000 of the congressional appropriation to Fort Jefferson. Some of the reasons for the sudden prioritization of defensive works were revealed by Brigadier General Totten in a confidential letter dated March 22, 1855, and addressed to all superintending engineers. Tensions with Spain had reached boiling point. Filibuster William Walker, referred to in some press accounts as "the grey-eyed man of destiny," created a diplomatic crisis for the United States with his military exploits in Nicaragua. Spain had also become aware of southern designs on Cuba and its possible annexation to the nation as another state where slavery, the "peculiar institution," would be legal. Due to the real possibility of war with Spain, General Totten wanted to ensure that all construction was clearly directed toward the ability of the forts to defend against attack. As the "key to the Gulf," and just ninety miles from Havana, Fort Jefferson was certainly one of the objects of warnings by the chief of engineers.[28]

Because of the slightly higher funding for 1854 the employment of white contract laborers had already reached a record high of 125 in February 1855.

Figure 2. Small howitzer embrasure in a lower bastion casemate. Photo by Paulien Reid.

Due to the crisis and increased funding, that number would peak at 233 in August 1855. Construction reports indicate that at the beginning of the surge the six bastions, or towers, at the corners of the walls were an average of two and one-half feet high. The curtain walls containing the casemates, or positions for the cannons, were on average five and one-half feet completed. As of the 1856 annual report all six bastions were at eight feet, and the casemates and walls were between ten and eleven feet in height. Once ammunition magazines and the arches over some of the casemates were completed, Fort Jefferson could mount the 115 smoothbore 42-pounder cannons proposed by General Totten for the first tier of guns. The engineer workforce, both black and white, had made remarkable progress.[29]

An anonymous article in *Putnam's Monthly Magazine* in March 1856, titled "Our Sea-Coast Defense and Fortification System," is probably typical of the engineers' pro-fortification information campaign that influenced the political landscape during the antebellum period. It reiterates the popular position of the 1821 Simon Bernard report of the Fortifications Board that such forts would allow the nation to maintain a small peacetime army by drawing wartime garrisons from militia in surrounding areas. The threat from an increasingly militarized Europe was stated forcefully in terms nearly identical to those used in the later reports of the Delafield Commission. The cost of completing works under construction was stated at $6.4 million, of which Fort Jefferson comprised 15 percent, or $989 thousand, the highest completion cost listed. The article concluded on a note of both nationalism and expansionism: "The commerce, whence our national revenue is almost entirely derived, is preeminently the interest served by our defenses, and may, with special justice, demand this protection. If we forecast the future of this commerce, and of all our national destiny, every vision of promised magnificence warns us to look well to those bulwarks of defense under cover of which we may safely ride out every storm of war."[30]

Numerous wrecks and groundings of ships on the reefs surrounding the Tortugas convinced the Treasury Department's Lighthouse Board that the light on Garden Key provided inadequate protection during foggy or inclement weather. It was decided that the best location for a taller light equipped with a brighter and more modern optical lens was on Loggerhead Key, site of one of the most dangerous reefs. A request for an estimate for the cost of the 150-foot tower was submitted to Captain Wright, superintending engineer at Fort Jefferson. Although he had no experience with the construction of lighthouse towers, Wright provided two possible designs in September 1855 with comparable costs of about $35,000. He recommended

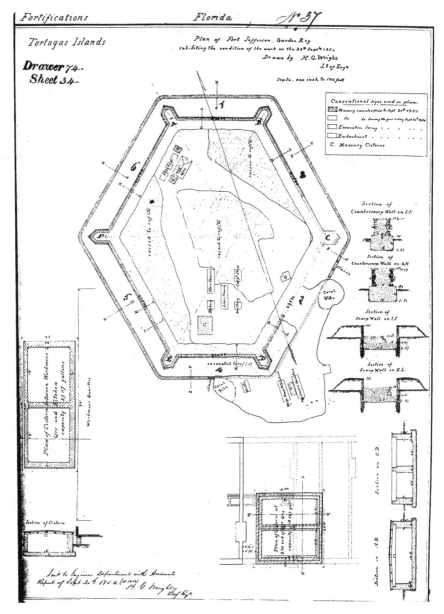

Figure 3. Graphic Progress Report on Construction submitted in 1854 by 1st Lieutenant Horatio G. Wright. Courtesy National Archives, Records Group 77 (Chief of Engineers), Drawer 74, Sheet 34.

Figure 4. Decorative pediment above exterior sallyport. Note the difference in size of Pensacola bricks in the lower courses and Maine bricks in courses above the pediment. "False embrasures" in the upper course gave ships the mistaken impression that the fort had three levels of gunrooms. Photo by Paulien Reid.

that local brick from Mobile or Pensacola should be used, noting that it was larger and more durable than brick available in New York.[31]

The actual construction of the Loggerhead light fell to Wright's replacement at Garden Key, Captain Daniel P. Woodbury, who had arrived and assumed his duties on March 22, 1856. Woodbury was a career soldier and 1836 U.S. Military Academy graduate. Initially commissioned to the Third U.S. Artillery regiment, he was assigned duties in support of the building of the National Road in Ohio. A short time later he was transferred to the Corps of Engineers in July 1837 and continued work on the National Road as the assisting engineer until 1840. Woodbury later completed a number of assignments in the West as well as two years acting as assistant to Chief of Engineers Joseph Totten in Washington, D.C. Prior to his transfer to Fort Jefferson, he had supervised the repair of coastal fortifications in North Carolina.[32] In addition to his duties on Garden Key, Captain Woodbury began supervising construction on the Loggerhead project as cooler weather (and workmen from the North) returned in October or November 1856.

The lighthouse tower was only a part of the planned construction. The site also included a nearby oil storage facility, a brick home for the keeper, brick cisterns for drinking water storage, and numerous outbuildings. Wright's design proved durable, for in spite of nearly a century and a half of hurricanes and tropical conditions the lighthouse tower is still in service. It was christened the Dry Tortugas Light and was first illuminated on July 1, 1858. The older sixty-five-foot tall lighthouse within the walls of Fort Jefferson was redesignated the Tortugas Harbor Light.[33] Most nineteenth-century accounts refer to the two as the Loggerhead Light and the Garden Key Light.

Shortly before the proposed construction of the new lighthouse was initiated, the Tortugas experienced the worst hurricane to strike the keys since work on Fort Jefferson had begun. Following a period of high thin clouds, intense heat, and absolute calm, heavy storm clouds gathered and intermittent rain began on August 27, 1856. The engineer schooner *Activa* was returning from a trip to Key West when increasingly intense winds forced the captain to seek a safe harbor on the lee side of the Marquesas Keys. By 5:00 p.m. the combination of high wind gusts and towering ocean swell snapped the anchor chain and set the ship adrift. The captain decided that the only remaining course of action was to make for the Tortugas under short sail. Following a laborious voyage of eight hours the crew spotted the Garden Key Light at about 3:00 a.m. Having no other option, the captain grounded the schooner on the reef at the nearest point to Fort Jefferson possible. Captain Ellis, his four-man crew, and one passenger safely reached the fort about dawn in the ship's boat. The storm continued well into the day of August 28. As the winds and rain abated, damage to construction was found to be limited to some missing slate on the roof of the officer quarters and several barrels of cement ruined by storm water. The schooner *Activa* had broken up on the reef and was a total loss. One of the flat barges used to transport sand and coral rock met a similar fate on nearby Long Key, half of which had been swept away by the storm.[34]

A more damaging setback struck Fort Jefferson during the night of May 15, 1857. Benjamin Kerr was refilling the twenty-three aging oil lamps of the Garden Key Light when he noticed that one of the engineer storehouses was on fire. Although the workmen were awakened and made a genuine effort to extinguish the blaze, the wooden frame structure was completely destroyed. A recently arrived shipload of tools, construction materials, and food valued at $7,000 were lost along with the building. Captain Woodbury reported the misfortune to the chief of engineers, speculating that the cause of the fire had been the "spontaneous combustion of tar and oil stored in the structure." He requested authorization to replace the warehouse with materials on hand. Five of the completed casemates would temporarily be boarded in and used for storage.[35]

In an effort to produce bricks of high enough quality and in sufficient quantity to satisfy their government contract to supply brick for Fort Jefferson and Fort Taylor, the firm of Raiford and Abercrombie relocated twice, once from Mobile and again from a brickyard on Escambia Bay. In 1857 Raiford sold his interest in the concern and the firm was subsequently known as Bacon and Abercrombie. Although the clay at the final location near Pensacola was of an ideal consistency and contained little sand, the company hired and dismissed a number of supervisors in a search for one who had the technical abilities necessary to meet the standards of the engineers building Forts Taylor and Jefferson.[36]

Demand for brick and labor for the project was so great that special machinery was designed and built to meet the need and to reduce labor costs. Patented with the assistance of the journal *Scientific American*, the "machine is the invention of a man who has been engaged for many years in the manufacture of brick on an extensive scale. Having a large contract for furnishing brick to be used in the construction of Fort Jefferson—the largest fortification in the United States, situated on the Island of Tortugas, off the coast of Florida—he had one of these machines constructed, and has subjected it to a thorough test. He says . . . it will turn out 40,000 bricks per day." The date of patent was August 17, 1858, and the inventor, John W. Crary, was employed by Bacon and Abercrombie at Pensacola, Florida, a location from which he maintained close contact with the builders. Bricks produced by the pressing process were tested by army engineers at the construction site and found to be superior to ordinary brick in "strength and power of resisting pressure." As a result of the automated process, the large number of slaves required to run the operation could have been reduced by more than half.[37] However, due to the timing of this automation, congressional appropriations, and the outbreak of sectional strife in 1861, the experiment was finally a failure.[38]

In a rare departure from engineer orthodoxy, Lieutenant James St. Clair Morton, later superintending engineer at Fort Jefferson, in 1858 submitted to Secretary of War John B. Floyd a long critique of the existing coastal defense posture.[39] Morton's attack on the official policy of his own branch was likely a response to Secretary of War Jefferson Davis's 1857 report to the president. Davis, guided by the observations gained by Major Richard

Figure 5. Second tier bastion casemates with compound arches designed by supervising engineer Daniel Woodbury and constructed 1856–58; photo circa 1900. Courtesy National Archives, 200M90-1-11.

Delafield and Captain George B. McClellan during the Crimean War, had described the failure of the most modern naval armaments against "properly constructed fortifications" such as those being built on the American coast. Davis had also echoed the theme in a second Delafield report—that an attack on the United States by a European power was probably inevitable.[40] Lieutenant Morton's conclusions that ever larger and more accurate naval guns demanded changes in traditional military architecture were generally ignored by both his peers and superiors.

Lieutenant Morton's departure from the widely accepted view that casemated masonry fortifications or "castles" were the answer to the nation's defensive needs emerge in part in a letter addressed to Secretary of War John B. Floyd in January 1858. The letter solicited permission to reorder the priorities for the defense of New York City. A series of inexpensive earthworks, both entrenchments and batteries, would be added to protect the city from an enemy landing by providing defensive positions for the militia. The changes in funding were approved and executed. While the modifications were not major and impacted only one site, the doctrinal departures from the Third or "Totten" System of permanent masonry structures certainly were significant.[41]

In a second communication with Secretary Floyd in October 1859 Morton proposed a near total break with the status quo and the published positions of the ranking officers of the Corps of Engineers. He proposed a new doctrine: "That each generation should build and pay for its own defenses and reap the benefit of them." Morton questioned the value the nation had received for past expenditures of $30 million and ongoing funding of $2 million a year that had produced a series of incomplete and indefensible forts. His recommendation was to terminate construction on unfinished works and complete their defenses with earthwork batteries. Morton exempted installations like Fort Jefferson and Fort Taylor since they "occupy . . . remote situations." His plan also suggested increased use of defensive torpedoes to mine harbors, including electrical command detonation by the defenders.[42] Although Lieutenant Morton's ideas had a great deal of merit, no support for them ever developed in Congress.

Secretary of War Floyd in particular had become a firm disciple of the Totten system of fortifications. In his 1858 report to Congress he was clear in his support: "Upon the general system of sea coast defense it is hardly necessary to say a word at this day. The policy of the government seems to be fixed in that respect, and wisely too, no doubt, if the works be prosecuted with a wise economy. Fortifications are now very justly esteemed the cheapest and far the most effectual means of defense for every important commercial point; with the heavy guns of the present day, no fleet can match a fortification, and when completed, these works can be kept in perfect repair at a very trifling cost."[43]

By 1859 progress on the construction of Fort Jefferson was impressive, though the structure remained incomplete. Nearly three hundred white workmen and local slaves were employed. The white workmen were primarily Irish immigrant laborers from New York. The resident physician, Dr. Daniel Whitehurst of Key West, announced his intention to retire after serving there for several years both as a doctor and as the engineer clerk. Several prominent naturalists had visited the Tortugas, including John James Audubon in 1832 and Louis Agassiz in the winter of 1858. They came away with glowing accounts of the research that could be conducted there in ornithology and marine biology. It was determined that the next physician should be one who combined the skills of a doctor and a scientist. Agassiz and Professor Spencer F. Baird of the Smithsonian Institution in Washington recommended their friend Joseph Basset Holder of Lynn,

Figure 6. View to the southwest from the top of bastion A. Ruins of the officer quarters and kitchen buildings can be seen on the parade. Photo by Paulien Reid.

Massachusetts, who had the desired qualifications as a zoologist as well as having completed his training at Harvard Medical School about 1850. The ultimate decision was probably made by Chief of Engineers Brig. Gen. Joseph G. Totten, who had been a regent of the Smithsonian since its founding in 1846.[44]

Dr. Holder accepted the position and began the long journey from Massachusetts to the most distant of the Florida Keys with his wife Emily and eight-year-old son Charles in the fall of 1859. The first leg of the trip from New York to Charleston, South Carolina, was made by rail, progress seeming slower and slower as they traveled farther south. At Charleston they boarded the *Isabel*, a steamer bound for Havana. The doctor and his family disembarked at Key West, where they were met by the engineer schooner *Tortugas*, which completed the journey to the fort on Garden Key at dawn the next day.

The Holders initially enjoyed the hospitality of the resident engineer, Captain Woodbury, and his family, but later they were provided with a small house within the confines of Fort Jefferson's parade field. Dr. Holder immediately assumed his medical duties at the engineer hospital located on the acre or so of the island outside the towering masonry walls of the fort. The carpenters built an extension on one of the waterfront structures that reached fifteen feet over the shallow lagoon. It served as a laboratory where

Holder could confine various marine organisms and observe their growth and development.

Emily Holder recorded her first impressions of the Tortugas: "The exterior of the fort was bare and repulsive, the interior offering a decided contrast. Here were trees of the deep green belonging to tropical vegetation, so restful to the eye in the glaring sun; and as the walls inclosed about thirteen acres, and water could not be seen, I instinctively lost the feeling of being so far from the mainland. The walk, hard as cement and white as snow, partly shaded by the evergreen trees, led past the lighthouse and cottage of the keeper to the opposite side of the fort."[45]

Garden Key residents from the North had to acclimate themselves to considerably more than the heat, violent thunderstorms, and high winds that plagued the tropics during the late summer months. Northern ladies also had to become accustomed to dealing with slaves, the only domestic servants available. Dr. and Mrs. Holder were permitted to hire Aunt Eliza, a woman well past her prime who had spent her youth in the cotton fields of South Carolina. Aunt Eliza was the property of Mrs. Fogarty, an immigrant from Ireland who ran the mess hall for the workmen. Stooped and missing her front teeth, Eliza covered her hair with a bright yellow turban. She described herself as having been too ugly to work in her master's house as a young girl and was evidently quite pleased to find herself mistress of the Holders' kitchen, which occupied a small separate building behind the house. Aunt Eliza shocked Emily Holder by smoking tobacco, a habit she attempted to hide at first by secreting her pipe in any number of inappropriate places among the crockery and in the pantry or by blaming the lingering odor on her boyfriend Jack. Emily's brisk Yankee efficiency in the kitchen during the oppressive heat of August failed to inspire Aunt Eliza to greater speed or alacrity but only elicited the comment that she was "stagnated."

As the late summer of 1859 dragged on "even Aunt Eliza began to tire of the Tortugas." She declared herself to be in a "low-down state," and "de only one lef' of all her family." When questioned, she admitted that her brothers were all still alive in Savannah but said she would probably never see them again. Eliza then admitted that "she would 'not las' long herself. 'De rheumatiz got above my knees now.' Then she would take her pipe and smoke until she was dizzy." The old slave lived in a room above the kitchen with her "husband" Jack, one of the slaves employed by the engineers. Jack was twenty years her junior and was tolerated only as long as he "waited upon her." Mrs. Holder also soon discovered that the slaves would eat everything on hand in the kitchen if not forbidden to do so in the strongest

Figure 7. Small two-story kitchen buildings were used by Dr. Holder and his family and engineer officers as quarters both before and during the war. Photo by Paulien Reid.

possible terms. The difficult introduction to life in the Gulf and the South's "peculiar institution" was relieved by lower temperatures in early October, which probably also lifted Aunt Eliza's "stagnation." Occasional trips by the Holders to enjoy the larger society of Key West provided diversion and relief.[46]

Because of Dr. Holder's dual role as the engineers' physician and as a zoologist nominally responsible to the Smithsonian and later the American Museum of Natural History, most family outings involved sailing among the nearby keys collecting samples and making observations. These studies were later published in two serialized articles, "Along the Florida Reef" and "The Dry Tortugas." The Holders' young son, Charles Frederick, was his father's constant companion on these explorations. He had been withdrawn from the doubtless strict confines of the Friends' School in Providence, Rhode Island, a Quaker boarding school previously attended by his father, and set free in the tropics with his parents as tutors. The effect of the experience gave Charles a lasting interest in nature and zoology, fields he pursued all of his adult life. At the age of eight, however, his attention was probably riveted by the warm Gulf, strange marine creatures, and the lighthouse keepers' stories of pirate treasure. Had it not been for the very real threat of deadly tropical diseases, the environment would have been nearly ideal for a young family.

The employment of slaves by the engineers had both practical and political components. Unlike white workmen from New York, the slaves, primarily from Key West, were mostly immune to tropical disease due to their exposure as children. For that reason, they could be employed year-round while the workers from the North generally refused to remain during the "sickly season" of June through October. Key West native and U.S. Senator Stephen Mallory, who owned a number of slaves working at Garden Key, complained to the secretary of war and alleged that the engineers' hiring practices gave preference to "Yankee artisans." The issue was referred to Captain Woodbury, who agreed that the acclimated local workers should be given preference in hiring and indicated that he had, in fact, increased the number of slaves on the payroll from forty to fifty-six during his tenure.[47]

The exchange between Senator Mallory and the engineers was quite civil in comparison to the slavery debate at the national level. Chief Justice Roger B. Taney wrote a majority opinion in *Dred Scott v. Sandford* declaring that Scott had no standing to bring a suit, since he was not a citizen but private property. Taney also wrote that in considering admission of territories Congress had no right to forbid slavery, since such property was recognized and protected under the Constitution. The decision was calculated to cause further polarization between America's proslavery and antislavery factions. In October 1859 John Brown and his radical abolitionist followers seized the United States arsenal at Harpers Ferry, Virginia, in an attempt to trigger and arm a slave rebellion in the South. A siege resulted in the death of ten of Brown's men when the armory was surrounded by militia and regular army troops. Capture and a trial for treason against the State of Virginia swiftly followed; Brown and six surviving followers were hanged in December 1859. Many southerners were convinced that antislavery forces had gained the upper hand in the North and that Brown's actions were evidence of a broad conspiracy against their interests.

A Union Threatened and
the Outbreak of War

1860–1861

Construction at Fort Jefferson continued at a slightly slower rate during 1860, primarily due to a reduced level of funding. Congress appropriated $95,000 on March 3, 1859 for work at Garden Key in fiscal year 1860.[1] The annual construction report for the year ending June 30, 1860, noted that the stair towers had progressed to the level of the second casemates, the curtain walls were between thirty and thirty-two feet in height, eighty-six of the second tier casemates had been completed, and granite steps had been set in the stair towers. Ammunition magazines in the six bastions had been projected for that year's construction by Captain Woodbury, but were omitted in the report and evidently were not completed.[2]

Typical of slave owners in the South, those at Key West were constantly vigilant in case of a mass escape or an uprising. Because of its isolation Fort Jefferson was believed to be a safe environment for slaves. In January 1860, however, Key West's slave owners were thrown into a panic by an entirely baseless rumor that the slaves at Garden Key had somehow all escaped to Nassau in the Bahamas. Captain Woodbury assured the owners that the report was false. The whites in the Tortugas were nevertheless apprehensive, and the atmosphere was not improved by allegations that the slave who assisted the blacksmith had been forging spear points in his leisure hours. The hysteria subsided as all of the rumors were proved untrue.[3]

Woodbury was called to Washington at the end of April and served on a working group that reviewed the plans for a number of other fortifications. Before departing on April 27, Woodbury placed chief overseer George Phillips in charge of the project. On the way from the Tortugas he took the opportunity to spend two weeks helping his family settle into their new home in Wilmington, Delaware, before proceeding to Washington. Reporting to headquarters in mid-May, he probably returned to Fort Jefferson in late June.[4] Work generally slowed during the summer months when many of the white workmen went home to avoid the intense heat and recurring outbreaks of yellow fever. The census of Garden Key taken in September 1860 listed only thirty free white inhabitants, including the Holders and their nine-year-old son Charles.[5]

The departure of Captain Woodbury and his family left the Holders more or less isolated on the remote key. Emily recalled: "They were sad days before and after Captain Woodbury's family left, for it took some time to adjust ourselves to the loneliness that followed; and I never shall forget the peculiar sensation with which I watched the schooner Tortugas float away with them all one bright moonlight night, leaving us almost alone upon this sand bank on the borders of the great Gulf Stream. The Fourth of July 1860 passed very quietly. Our greatest annoyances now were the delay of the mails and the scarcity of good things to eat. We wearied of canned food, and pined for fresh vegetables."[6]

Montgomery C. Meigs, captain of engineers and the original architect of Fort Jefferson, left Washington, D.C., on October 22, 1860, and traveled overland through the South to assume charge of the construction of the fort he had designed. The assignment to the Tortugas, however, was an exile, not a desirable assignment. Meigs had graduated from the U.S. Military Academy in 1836 and had quickly become a prodigy, not only in terms of civil engineering but also in operating at the heights of political power. Under the aegis of Secretary of War Jefferson Davis and President Franklin Pierce, Captain Meigs was entrusted in 1853 with the completion of the United States Capitol building as well as the construction of the Washington Aqueduct. Seven years later, he repeatedly clashed with President James Buchanan's new secretary of war, John B. Floyd, over a range of ethical issues and attempts by Floyd to use the construction projects in Washington to reward political cronies. In the final analysis, Meigs's integrity was not compromised, but Floyd retained his position in Washington, and the young engineer was on his way to one of the most remote and isolated posts in the nation.[7]

At the time of his reassignment the majority of the construction material used on Garden Key was purchased in Pensacola, a market and suppliers with which he was unfamiliar. Since a shortcoming in materials could easily contribute to contracting problems, Meigs requested that Captain Daniel Woodbury, the current superintending engineer for Fort Jefferson, accompany him and make necessary introductions. His request was ap-

Figure 8. Unfinished separate ammunition magazine with northeast curtain 1 and bastion A to the right. Photo by Paulien Reid.

proved by the acting chief of engineers, Lieutenant Colonel Rene DeRussy, and Woodbury was directed to return with Meigs by way of Pensacola to the Tortugas, where a formal transfer of records and responsibility would be conducted.[8]

On their way they passed through Knoxville, Tennessee, Columbus, Georgia, and Montgomery, Alabama. At Pensacola Woodbury made introductions at the firm of Bacon and Abercrombie, the manufacturer of the majority of bricks being used at Fort Jefferson at that time, as well as taking Meigs to meet smaller suppliers of lumber, lime, Portland cement, and provisions.[9] Meigs and Woodbury then took passage aboard the mail steamer and arrived at Key West on November 7 and Garden Key in the Dry Tortugas on November 8. Meigs was disturbed by the angry attitudes he had encountered along his way. He then took what for a professional officer was a bold action when, on November 10, he wrote a personal letter to Lieutenant General Winfield Scott, the senior general officer in the army. Meigs stated: "I found on some parts of the route a very strong feeling of hostility to the Union. . . . About Columbus, Ga., and Montgomery, Ala., I gather that this feeling of disloyalty to the Union is particularly rife." Although he did not yet know the outcome of the election, he observed that "resistance to the inauguration or to the administration of a Republican President has been openly discussed." Meigs suggested to General Scott that "wise discretion and preparation" might preclude a later requirement for military action.[10]

Captain Meigs pointed out in some detail the near total lack of military readiness of major installations at Pensacola, Key West, and at Garden Key. At the latter, he reported there was "not a single gun," and in terms of small arms, it was doubtful that six shotguns could be mustered. This was in spite of the fact that construction had proceeded to the point that a large number of guns could be mounted and sufficient quantities of ammunition could be stored there.

> The embrasures of the lower tier are ready for their guns. Magazines exist for ammunition. The walls are thirty feet in height, and the armament of the flanks by a few carronades or howitzers and the placing of one or two heavy guns on each curtain, with a proper supply of ammunition and small-arms, would enable a single company of artillery, with the aid of the volunteers who could be gathered from the wrecking and fishing fleet in these waters and from the workmen and others here employed, to hold this extensive and important work against any such expedition, and the fact that the work was thus prepared would be sufficient to prevent any attempt upon it.

Meigs concluded: "At present both this place and Fort Taylor [Key West] are at the mercy of [an enemy] party which could be transported in a fishing smack. What a disgrace such an assault, if successful, would inflict upon our Government."[11]

Captain Meigs was not idle in his efforts to improve the security and defensibility of the installations in the Keys. On November 15, 1860, he wrote to Captain Thomas Craven, the commander of the Key West naval station as well as captain of the armed steamship *Mohawk*, relating his concerns and requesting naval support for Forts Taylor and Jefferson. Meigs explained, "I look for no expedition authorized by the constituted authorities of any State, but any small party of men anxious to embroil the different sections of the Union might find a tempting bait in either of these important fortresses." Craven was in agreement with Meigs and directed a second steamship, the *Wyandotte*, to provide support for Fort Taylor while he sailed aboard the *Mohawk* to lie off the Tortugas. About two weeks later,

Craven received a message from President Buchanan's secretary of the navy, Isaac Toucey, that "the Department does not, from any information in its possession, deem it necessary that you should remain at the Tortugas to guard Fort Jefferson." He ordered Craven to return to Key West.[12]

As tensions increased following Abraham Lincoln's election, Scott evidently took the engineer's warnings seriously. On December 28, 1860, he wrote to Secretary of War John B. Floyd to

> ask the attention of the Secretary to Forts Jefferson and Taylor, which are wholly national, being of far greater value even to the most distant points of the Atlantic coast and to the people on [the Mississippi and its tributaries] than to the State of Florida. There is only a feeble company at Key West for the defense of Fort Taylor, and not a soldier in Fort Jefferson to resist a handful of filibusters or a rowboat of pirates; and the Gulf, soon after the beginning of secession or revolutionary troubles in the adjacent States, will swarm with such nuisances."[13]

The secretary had little time to consider the validity of General Scott's position. John B. Floyd resigned the next day, December 29.[14]

Scott evidently gave his approval for some initial defensive actions, and Army Headquarters began directing troop movements accordingly. On January 4, 1861, Lieutenant Colonel G. W. Lay, Scott's aide-de-camp, directed Captain John M. Brannan of the First U.S. Artillery to move his company from Key West Barracks to Fort Taylor. He was ordered to "consult with the commander of any United States man-of-war in the harbor, and invite his co-operation. . . . If necessary for [your defense] you may take one or two boxes of the muskets shipped in the *Water Witch* intended for Capt. Meigs."[15] At Fort Independence in Boston Harbor, Major Lewis G. Arnold reported to the War Department that he had received the "Orders of the General-in-Chief by telegraph" and would embark the afternoon of January 10 aboard the steamer *Joseph Whitney* with four officers and sixty-two enlisted men of the Second U.S. Artillery Regiment. Arnold's orders stated that if Fort Jefferson was being held by Rebel forces that could not be dislodged, he was to proceed to Fort Taylor at Key West and take command there. The officers with Major Arnold included a surgeon, Adam N. McLaren.[16] Secretary of the Navy Toucey was also aware of the urgency of the situation and sent encoded instructions to the commander of the U.S.S. *Crusader* at Pensacola to "proceed immediately to Garden Key and cooperate with commanding officer to protect public property and prevent anyone from landing improperly."[17]

The mission directing Major Arnold to garrison Garden Key was unknown to Captain Meigs, and he still had serious concerns about the security of the outposts in the Keys following the departure of the *Mohawk*. In one letter he mused: "Well I hope that no hot headed South Carolinian will head a dozen fire eaters some bright night through the open gaps in the wall of what ought to be Fort Jefferson to astonish me in bed by demanding a surrender in the name of the Great Moloch & the Southern Congress."[18] Meigs's speculations might have taken on a more nightmarish tone had he been aware that the State of South Carolina had seceded from the Union on December 20. News was slow in arriving at the Tortugas.

In Florida a state convention met on January 10, 1861, and soon adopted an ordinance of secession removing the state from the Union and declaring it a "sovereign and independent nation." Rebels quickly seized naval stores and forts on the mainland at Pensacola. U.S. Army Lieutenant Adam J. Slemmer, recognizing the threat to government facilities, abandoned Fort McRee on the mainland and, with eighty men, occupied the much more defensible Fort Pickens on Santa Rosa Island. Lincoln's secretary of the navy, Gideon Welles, later wrote: "This post, with Fort Jefferson at the Dry Tortugas, and Fort Taylor at Key West—the two last lying off the Florida coast—remained in possession of the Government when the change of administration took place on the 4th of March." The momentum of the secession movement grew, and by February six southern states had withdrawn from the Union. The federal authorities had entered into an unwritten understanding with "certain rebel leaders" that Florida would abstain from any actions to extend its authority over the forts of the United States "provided the Federal Government would in the mean time remain inactive."[19]

Captain Meigs and the contractors at Fort Jefferson worked feverishly to improve the defensive posture of the post. On January 15, 1861, he submitted his routine construction report for December along with a lengthy letter to the Engineer Corps in Washington. He noted that workers had "closed nearly 200 openings in the scarp wall, taken up several bridges which gave easy access to the work, put up a draw bridge and a gate at the postern, and brought the work into a condition which would enable a small force with guns and supplies to hold it." Meigs was forced to conclude that in spite of his efforts, "unless it is soon occupied by the United States in proper force I have no doubt that it will be seized by the parties who have shown so much more energy and promptness than . . . the Army and Navy of the United States." The letter was forwarded through Havana, since mail could no longer be sent through an area in open rebellion.[20]

Figure 9. Fort Jefferson sallyport with guardrooms to left and right. Photo by Paulien Reid.

Emily Holder recalled the growing tension and the defenseless posture of the post:

> Active work began on our return [from Key West]. A drawbridge was made and raised every night, all communication with the outside being cut off. The evening of the seventeenth of January Captain Meigs called, and I remember his reading Shakespeare aloud, and discussing some of the historical plays with my husband. They were both students of Shakespeare. In the midst of it Mr. Howells came in saying that the sheriff had arrived from Key West to arrest the fishermen, and they had sent for Captain Meigs to intercede for them.

The facts of the case were that the State of Florida had made a new law that none of the fishermen could obtain a clearance to go to Havana without paying a fine or license of two or three hundred dollars. Of course they could not pay it; and the object was to drive them home. They were mostly from Connecticut; and there were fourteen smacks in the harbor. They came down every winter to fish, taking their catch to Havana market.

Captain Meigs sent word to them not to pay it, and to the sheriff that he was governor of that island, and he had better return to Key West. Then he sent Mr. Howells off privately that night to Key West for guns. He felt it was time to take the responsibility, even if he was censured for it.[21]

Captain Meigs's frustration was evident in his January 17 letter to Captain Brannan, commander of Fort Taylor at Key West. Meigs complained strongly that officials of the State of Florida were not only charging fishing vessels fees at the U.S. Customs facility at Key West but that the Monroe County fishery commissioner had arrived with a sheriff at Fort Jefferson and that fishermen in port there from other states had "been compelled to pay fees amounting to $210 for each smack over thirty tons." That, Meigs insisted, was an affront to his status as a U.S. commissioner and commanding officer of the islands, which were federal property. He then came to the point and admitted that he was in no position to enforce federal law without any armaments. "Under these circumstances, I send a special messenger to you to ask the loan of six flanking guns . . . and of six heavy casemate guns, with their implements and ammunition. The vessel which carries this letter can bring back the small guns, and one of those about the fort could doubtless be chartered to bring the others."[22]

Due to the agreement between the Buchanan administration and the Florida secessionists, the troops and supplies sent to reinforce Fort Pickens and Fort Taylor remained on board their transports within sight of their goals. No such diplomatic hesitation was necessary regarding the still unarmed Fort Jefferson, lying over one hundred miles off the Florida coast. Observation of the landing of troops and ordnance was unlikely. On January 18, 1861, Major Arnold and his company arrived at Garden Key aboard the steamer *Joseph Whitney*. Arnold relieved Captain Meigs, who had been in no position to defend the site. At that time the island was home to the lighthouse keeper, his family, and fifty laborers. Many of the latter were slaves contracted to the government by their owners at Key West. Major

Figure 10. View looking northeast toward bastion C, showing the counterscarp (seawall), sallyport, and bridge; photo May 1898. Courtesy National Archives, 200 M90-3B-86.

Arnold wrote a letter that same day to the adjutant general indicating that he had garrisoned the post and assumed command.[23] The arrival of the steamer had caused a great deal of anxiety on the part of both the defenders and their reinforcements, since neither the fort nor the ship flew any flag. Major Arnold sent the ship's first mate and Lieutenant Benson ashore in a small boat to determine the status of the fort. "The relief of Captain Meigs and party may be supposed of receiving the agreeable information that the steamer contained reinforcements with the view of preserving the fort to the United States."[24]

Captain Meigs wrote a lengthy report the next day to Brigadier General Joseph G. Totten, the chief engineer, in Washington. He proudly stated that "the work is now secure to the United States, and I trust that its flag once raised upon these walls will never again be lowered." Meigs assured the general that the new soldiers would be well cared for. "For the present garrison I have made provisions in some of the frame buildings, erected within the fort as quarters, storehouses, &c., and some few days' work will accomplish all that is necessary for their healthful and comfortable accommodation."[25]

A description of the fort in January 1861 included details on the progress of its construction and defenses:

> This fortification extends over the whole surface of Garden Key, and has an area over thirteen acres. It is completely closed against surprise by escalade, though its armament is incomplete. The first and second tiers, however, are finished, and the twelve outworks of bastions and curtains can mount three hundred and fifty guns. The fort is further fortified by a wide ditch, reaching to the water, and protected by a strong counterscarp. The guns of the fort command the inner harbor, but the outer bay is beyond their longest range. The whole armament for the fort, when complete, is 450 guns, and the garrison necessary for its defense 1,000 men.[26]

The article neglected to say that at the time of Major Arnold's arrival there were no cannons of any description on Garden Key. Requisitions were quickly sent aboard the *Joseph Whitney* to Fort Taylor for guns, powder, and ammunition. The ship docked at Key West on January 20. Major Arnold reported that First Lieutenant Henry Benson and Captain Meigs returned on January 23 with "six 8-inch colombiads (smoothbore cannons) and four field pieces and an ample supply of ammunition, which, with the two field pieces I brought from Fort Independence, will enable me as soon as they are in position to make a strong defense, most probably to hold this important position—the key of the Gulf—against any force that is likely to be brought against it."[27] When the large guns were unloaded the artillerymen mounted them on expedient carriages made from construction timbers.

When they arrived at Key West to load the ordnance, Captain Meigs had been informed of a rumor that five hundred men had allegedly sailed from New Orleans with designs on the Florida Keys. Meigs wrote to General Totten that if the Rebels had designs on Fort Jefferson, they could expect to be "warmly welcomed if their appearance and conduct deserve it."[28] Thomas A. Craven, commanding the U.S.S. *Mohawk*, was informed of the rumor, left Key West and sailed to the Tortugas, where he remained until the heavy guns arrived and were mounted.[29] The rumored ship from New Orleans arrived at the Tortugas on the same day that Lieutenant Benson and Captain Meigs returned from Key West with the guns. The ship was the U.S. Mail Steamer *Galveston*, and its captain informed Major Arnold that Governor

Thomas Moore of Louisiana had offered to send ten thousand volunteers to assist Florida in an assault on Forts Taylor and Jefferson but that very few men ever signed on to the expedition. Meigs reported that the threat had not materialized and assured the War Department that with Arnold's men and the seventy-five engineer workmen present, more guns could be manned if they were sent.[30]

Captain Meigs wrote a status update to General Totten on January 25, 1861, when the last of the new guns were mounted. One of the greatest concerns in the Dry Tortugas was a lack of fresh drinking water. Meigs reported that "we have for our present population of 168 persons, including all non-effective women, children, &c., 850 days' supply of pure water at the Navy [consumption] rates, and besides this a very large quantity of water in the cisterns in the casemates. Much of this is good for washing and cooking. Some of the cisterns, however, have never been made tight, and water in them is salt." He related that the rainwater runoff stored under the parade field was fresh. The water in the cisterns beneath the walls and gun emplacements, however, had passed through locally procured coral sand used as filler during construction. As a result, it had dissolved out salts that made it unfit to drink. Captain Meigs suggested that the large amount of sand required to "bombproof" the areas above arches and the ammunition storage bunkers should be brought from the mainland to ensure that it was free of salt. "Fine, white, siliceous sand could be obtained from the banks of some of the navigable fresh-water streams of the Everglades by contract at moderate rates."[31] The fact that the mainland was now in the hands of secessionist Rebels evidently had not penetrated the realm of engineering theory.

On a more practical note, Meigs reported that the guardhouse would be finished in a few days and that plans were under way for the construction of a new concrete wharf. "I propose, if I can get piles, to commence at once building a permanent wharf of concrete and to set up the iron crane so long since brought here by Captain Wright. This will enable us to land guns with much saving of labor and time." He expressed satisfaction that the essential structure of the fort had been completed and that he could devote his undivided attention to "assisting the artillery officers in preparing their batteries."[32] Major Arnold's personnel return of January 31, 1861, was the first to be filed with the Adjutant General's Office from Fort Jefferson. On that report he listed Dr. Adam McLaren, the post surgeon; First Lieutenants Henry Benson and Matthew M. Blunt; and Second Lieutenant Thomas E. Miller, who was absent on convalescent leave until May. Dr. McLaren had

Figure 11. Mounted 24-pounder flank defense howitzer in embrasure. Photo by Paulien Reid.

an enlisted assistant, hospital steward Joseph Otto. At the time of the report five soldiers were listed as sick.[33]

At Key West, Captain Brannan reported to Army Headquarters on February 6, 1861: "Nothing has occurred at Key West since my last communication to disturb my relations with its citizens. It is very doubtful now if any attempt will be made upon this fort. I have transferred seven more 8-inch colombiads to Major Arnold, which will give him additional strength if ammunition is furnished him by the Ordnance Department. My powder is very bad; also friction tubes [fuse igniters]. A supply should be sent here immediately."[34]

During a drill on January 26 the first of the heavy guns was fired at Garden Key. The powder and primers from Fort Taylor were so damp that twelve primers were required to fire two rounds. It was determined that the powder should be transferred into airtight metal containers to prevent further degradation.[35]

More guns were received at Garden Key and were mounted in the empty casemates. The sloop *Brooklyn* anchored briefly on February 2 to unload four mountain howitzers and then continued to Pensacola with another company of the First U.S. Artillery commanded by Captain Israel Vogdes to be stationed at Fort Pickens. Captain Meigs contracted for the brig *Alpine* to transport the seven 8-inch colombiads along with their carriages and gear from Fort Taylor.[36] Meigs and his colombiads arrived back at the Tortugas on February 9. "The addition of these cannon increased Fort Jefferson to thirteen 8-inch colombiads on carriages, twelve light flanking guns, five 12-pounder brass howitzers, and four mountain howitzers."[37] General Totten wrote telling Captain Meigs that the Ordnance Department would soon transfer thirty-six 8-inch colombiads and thirty-six 24-pounder howitzers complete with carriages for the work. Totten recommended that they should be mounted *en barbette* (on platforms) on the terreplien (roof) of each of the six bastions.[38]

On February 4, 1861, Major General David E. Twiggs, commander of the Department of Texas, sent a message to each post and garrison in the state, informing them that a convention had passed an ordinance of secession that would take effect on March 2. Twiggs added that he had made five requests for instructions to Washington and had received nothing in return. He instructed all commanders to remain alert and to be prepared to move on short notice. General Twiggs, a native of Georgia, did not inform his subordinates that he had submitted his resignation and intended to offer his services to the Confederacy.[39]

The general-in-chief was determined that the artillery stationed on the Mexican border would not fall into the hands of the Texas secessionists. Orders were dispatched three days later on February 7 to Colonel C. A. Waite, Twiggs's replacement and the new department commander, ordering all remaining U.S. troops to meet a steamer transport then on its way to the port of Brazos Santiago near the southern end of Padre Island. An intended sense of urgency was added by instructions to load the guns and abandon their horses at the port. A separate order was sent to Brevet Major William H. French at Fort Duncan, near Eagle Pass, Texas, ordering him to evacuate the post, take command of the three companies of artillery at Fort Duncan and two at Fort Brown, and to embark at Brazos Santiago. Major French was further directed to land Batteries L and M of the First U.S. Artillery at Fort Jefferson in the Tortugas and to accompany Batteries F and K to Fort Taylor on Key West, where he would take command.[40]

These Union forces escaped from Texas by a narrow margin. On February 18 General Twiggs agreed to withdraw his troops and issued General Order no. 5, surrendering all federal property in the state to Brigadier General Ben McCulloch, the military representative of the Secession Convention. The posts on the Rio Grande were seized by Colonel John S. "Rip" Ford, named as commander of an expedition to "demand the surrender of Fort Brown and the public property belonging to the same." A force of fifteen hundred Texan militia camped near the port of Brazos Santiago ensured compliance with the terms of the surrender.[41] Major French and his artillerymen embarked aboard the steamships *Daniel Webster* and *General Rusk* on March 20, 1861, marking the official abandonment of Forts Brown and Duncan.[42]

Evacuating French and his field batteries was extremely difficult. The steamships could not cross the submerged sandbar into the port. Barrels of drinking water, soldiers, and guns had to be shuttled in small lighters or shallow draft ships. Knowing of the problems with the port, Major Fitz John Porter had been sent by the War Department aboard the *Daniel Webster* with $40,000 to hire lighters or charter ships as needed. From March 3 until March 13 operations were prevented by rough surf and high winds. Porter reported: "Only one lighter crosses the bar at Brazos Santiago, and the owner could not be induced to risk his vessel by the side of the *Webster* or any other side-wheel steamer, or to anchor sufficiently near to embark any portion of the battery or luggage, or even to transfer troops, unless the sea became very smooth." Once conditions grew calm a second vessel, "an old, very small schooner," was hired. Porter finally completed loading the last field guns and soldiers a week later on March 20.[43]

Because of his decisive services during the secession crisis and his greater experience, Captain Meigs was ordered on February 13 to replace First Lieutenant James St. C. Morton as superintending engineer on the construction of the Washington Aqueduct. Secretary of War Floyd had resigned in December under a cloud of allegations. Morton and Meigs exchanged assignments immediately. Temporary charge of the work at Garden Key was left with Lieutenant Chauncey B. Reece, a recent arrival at Fort Jefferson from New Orleans. Meigs wasted no time, departing on the engineer schooner *Tortugas* the same day the order arrived; the ship stopped briefly in Havana for coal and sailed for Washington on February 15. Meigs was back in the capital by the evening of February 20.[44] Morton relieved Reece of his supervisory duties on April 1, when Reece became his assistant.[45]

Lieutenant Morton, now the superintending engineer on Garden Key, reported to the chief of engineers that he and the two companies of the First Artillery from Texas arrived on March 24. Morton was concerned because Major Arnold, the post commander, had ordered him to change his construction priorities and concentrate on the barracks for the garrison. This began an unproductive turf war between Arnold and General Totten, the chief of engineers, centered on the issue of using funds from a congressional construction appropriation for an unintended purpose. Lincoln's newly appointed secretary of war, Simon Cameron, finally ruled against the engineers and came down on the side of common sense. Lieutenant Morton was directed to use the funds to construct permanent quarters for Arnold's artillerymen.[46]

Personnel returns for March indicated that Surgeon McLaren departed with the *Daniel Webster* to return to New York with Battery M of the Second U.S. Artillery. He was replaced by Assistant Surgeon W. J. L'Engle, who had been serving in Texas at Fort Brown. The addition of Batteries L and M of the First Artillery to the Fort Jefferson garrison raised the number of soldiers stationed at Garden Key to 244. The two batteries from Texas were commanded by Captain Samuel K. Dawson and First Lieutenant Lewis O. Morris. The Texas contingent also added four musicians and four farriers and blacksmiths to the post.[47]

The late January 1861 incident that may have been the only threatened Confederate attack on Fort Jefferson was described much later, in September 1905, by Brigadier General Loomis L. Langdon, formerly of the First U.S. Artillery. It does not occur in any of the official records of the period, although that in itself should not cause the account to be questioned.

> One afternoon as [Arnold] was anxiously supervising the working of his very first carriage, an armed privateer appeared off the fort and a message came ashore demanding the surrender of the fort to the State of Florida. To say Arnold nearly had a fit is to put it mildly. Of course the messenger had not been allowed to enter the fort, but sent in his message by the officer of the guard. Major Arnold rushed to the embrasure nearest the sally-port and shouted out to the man, "Tell your captain I will blow his ship out of water if he is not gone from here in ten minutes. [I] think I will open fire anyway." Within a few minutes the schooner was blending with the horizon.[48]

Following the inauguration of Abraham Lincoln on March 4, 1861, tensions continued to rise due to the standoff between federal troops besieged at Fort Sumter in Charleston Harbor and forces of the new Confederacy. President Lincoln and General-in-Chief Winfield Scott wanted to avoid a similar second possible flashpoint at Fort Pickens in Pensacola Bay. Brevet Colonel Harvey Brown of the Fifth U.S. Artillery was selected to reinforce the post with two companies of infantry, an artillery battery, and a company of the engineers' sappers and miners. Additionally, Brown would "assume command of all of the land forces of the United States within the State of Florida." Colonel Brown was also given an order signed by the president dated April 1, 1861. "All officers of the Army and Navy to whom this order may be exhibited," the order read, "will aid by every means in their power the expedition under the command of Col. Harvey Brown, supplying him with men and material, and co-operating with him as he may desire."[49] Armed with this highest possible authority, Brown sailed from New York aboard the transport steamship *Atlantic*. Captain Meigs accompanied Brown as chief engineer on the explicit orders of President Lincoln.[50]

The new commander of the Department of Florida arrived at Key West on April 12, unaware that Confederate forces had opened fire on Fort Sumter that same day. Colonel Brown ordered the loading of guns and supplies for his expedition from stocks at Fort Taylor. He also took thirty-three soldiers from the garrison "to fill vacancies caused by desertion or other absence at New York." The *Atlantic* left Key West on the morning of April 14 and arrived at Garden Key at 1:00 p.m. Colonel Brown found Fort Jefferson well defended and commended Major Arnold for his vigilance.

Brown also drew heavily on the post's limited assets: "I took from Fort Jefferson twenty negro laborers for the Engineer Department, thirty-one privates to fill up the companies, so that they are now full, a field battery and four mountain howitzers, with implements and ammunition, some bricks, and a large flat [barge]. We got under way at 8 o'clock p.m., and very soon lost the flat. Her lashing-rigs and hooks, not being sufficiently strong, drew out and left her adrift. Lieutenants McFarland and Reese, of the Engineers, on the advice of the chief engineer [Capt. Meigs], have been attached to this command."[51]

On April 15, 1861, Colonel Brown wrote to Major Arnold, "Your post may not improperly be considered the Gibraltar of America, and you should guard it with the same vigilance you would if we were at war with a strong maritime power."[52] This exhortation was followed by a long list of the preparations and standing orders that Arnold should have in place to ensure the safety and constant readiness of the soldiers and the necessary preparations to prevent any surprise by an enemy force. The orders were mostly advice concerned with matters that would have been second nature to any experienced professional officer—and were probably perceived by Arnold as poor compensation for his loss of guns, ammunition, soldiers, workers, and two engineer officers.

The removal of the contracted slaves to Fort Pickens by Colonel Brown caused a furor among their owners at Key West. Major French, the commander of Fort Taylor, recently arrived from Texas, wrote to Major Arnold April 20: "I have been with Lieutenant Morton, Engineer Corps, to the town of Key West, for the purpose of giving my personal guarantee that any negroes he may be able to engage for labor at your post will not be removed therefrom for any purpose whatever without the consent of their owners." Local slave owners were in a high state of excitement and had heated discussions regarding the "capture" of their bondsmen at Garden Key. Major French concluded that the results of the incident produced "difficulties not readily to be overcome."[53] The abduction of the slaves may have been an intentional affront to the slave owners of Key West. Captain Meigs was well aware that a number of them were the property of former Florida senator Stephen Mallory, who had become the Confederate secretary of the navy.[54]

Colonel Brown's decisive actions to ensure the defense of Fort Pickens had the effect of stirring up a hornet's nest of various parochial interests. Overall, however, his actions—closely coordinated with Captain Meigs, temporarily the chief engineer for the Department of Florida—had the desired effect of making the fort on Pensacola Bay nearly invulnerable to any threat that local Confederates could muster. One key to his success was coordination with the U.S. naval vessels in the area, the activities of which he placed in support of Fort Pickens and the installations in the Keys. On April 22 Brown informed Major Arnold that Virginia had seceded and that Rebels had seized the naval yard at Gosport as well as several large warships that were in port. Later that day in a second letter Colonel Brown told Arnold that the U.S.S. *St. Louis* had been ordered to the Tortugas to add a measure of protection if needed.[55] The fall of Fort Sumter to Confederate attackers marked the beginning of the war and triggered the secession not only of Virginia but of North Carolina, Tennessee, and Arkansas as well.

President Abraham Lincoln issued a proclamation on April 19, 1861, announcing a naval blockade of South Carolina, Georgia, Florida, Alabama, Mississippi, Louisiana, and Texas. This was extended on April 27 to include Virginia and North Carolina. An increased naval presence in the waters surrounding Fort Jefferson was immediate. The steamers *Brooklyn*, *Powhatan*, *Wyandotte*, *Crusader*, and *Mohawk* were quickly tasked as the Eastern Gulf Blockading Squadron operating from Pensacola and Key West. A third presidential proclamation on May 10, 1861, extended extraordinary powers to "the commander of the forces of the United States on the Florida coast to permit no person to exercise any office or authority upon the islands of Key West, the Tortugas, and Santa Rosa which may be inconsistent with the laws and Constitution of the United States, authorizing him at the same time, if he shall find it necessary, to suspend there the writ of habeas corpus, and to remove from the vicinity of the United States fortresses all dangerous or suspected persons."[56]

Prior to the attack on Fort Sumter Major Arnold was not convinced that war with the Confederacy was inevitable or unavoidable. He did believe, however, that Spain might attempt to take advantage of any weakness on the part of a divided United States by seizing offshore possessions in the Gulf of Mexico. Arnold coordinated with newly arrived Lieutenant Morton of the engineers to begin implementation of long neglected plans for the fortification of nearby islands that commanded the narrow channels approaching Fort Jefferson. Emily Holder noted: "The outside fortifications began with a breastwork on Bush Key, which hitherto had been the home of the sea-gull. The trees were cut and made into facines (woven branches to stabilize earthen walls). Sand Key was to have an [artillery] battery; and finally we learned that the fort was to become a naval station, vessels being on the way with stores." Lieutenant Morton bought all the wheelbarrows and shovels that could be found at Key West. He also requested a detachment of engineer sappers and miners and three hundred contract workmen from New York. Despite the arrival of summer and temperatures in the nineties, work progressed smoothly. In the course of their excavations a few feet offshore workers discovered a large, well-preserved cannon bearing the arms of England and the date of casting as 1700.[57]

By the end of April 1861 the garrison's armaments had been increased to forty-three 8-inch colombiads, eight field guns, and twenty-four 24-pounder howitzers. An ordinance sergeant, Christopher Slaven, had arrived on April 11 along with the fifty-four added heavy guns. Lieutenant James Morton, the superintending engineer, was listed on the return for the first time along with Assistant Surgeon Clinton Wagner, who arrived on April 22. Dr. L'Engle, the former assistant surgeon, had submitted his resignation and was on leave pending its approval.[58]

Despite the outbreak of open warfare between the United States and the Confederacy, the chief of engineers refused to drop the matter of what he believed were improper and high-handed acts perpetrated by Colonel Harvey Brown, commander of the Department of Florida, and Major Arnold, Brown's subordinate and commandant of Fort Jefferson. General Totten was particularly irritated by Arnold's redirecting the priorities of work on Garden Key that used federal construction funds appropriated by Congress. He complained to Army Headquarters in Washington: "The authorities will decide whether it is necessary to guard the special operations of the engineer department from such interference, or to protect disbursing engineers from the pecuniary difficulties that the execution of illegal orders must entail."[59] There is no record of Totten's reaction when he was informed that Colonel Brown was acting on the authority of the president of the United States.

First Lieutenant James Watts Robinson of Battery L, First U.S. Artillery, arrived at Fort Jefferson in March 1861 and soon found himself in a difficult position. A southerner and native of Virginia, he resigned his commission after learning that the Commonwealth had seceded from the Union in April. His resignation was accepted by the War Department on May 25, 1861. In order to prevent Robinson's possible commissioning in the Confederate Army and to retain his services, Major Arnold offered him the position of post sutler on Garden Key. Robinson, whose wife was a northerner, favorably considered the offer, and remained in that position for four years. Robinson recalled: "I never would have been in the position of sutler to the army but for Arnold's shrewdness and desire to keep me out of the Southern army. He made a neutral out of me as a soldier, but kept my energies on the Union side." While soldiers and officers often complained about the prices charged by sutlers, these provisioners provided a valuable service by selling tobacco, fresh and canned food, clothing items, and goods that would not otherwise have been available.[60] Robinson enjoyed the trust and support of each of the succeeding post commandants throughout the war and evidently provided a quality service to soldiers stationed there.

Despite the outbreak of war, life in the Tortugas retained a slow and peaceful pace. Seabirds returned by the thousands in May and June to nest. Although the engineers were busily constructing a defensive earthwork on Bird Key, the gulls were not discouraged and began the noisy process of selecting nesting sites and laying their eggs. The eggs were so numerous that the garrison at Garden Key could remove a flour barrel full without having any perceptible effect. Private Edward Hetherton of the Second Artillery, Company C, wrote: "We had plenty to eat at Fort Jefferson. Fish came in in great schools, and we waded in behind them and threw them to shore with our hands. There was a lighthouse on Loggerhead Island, where plenty of turtles were to be had. Arnold let us go there at times turtle-hunting."[61] On the night of July 1 Emily Holder reported seeing the "comet of '61 from the top of the fort. Its appearance was sublime, as it extended over nearly half of the heavens. The colored people were inclined to be superstitious; and many wondered if the world was not coming to an end."[62]

On July 4, 1861, the garrison's first volunteer reinforcements arrived aboard the steamer *State of Georgia* in the form of Companies B and E of Colonel Bill Wilson's Sixth New York Zouaves. This contingent joined Battery M of the First Artillery and Battery C of the Second Artillery. Wilson's Zouaves was a poorly trained unit drawn in large part from the coarser population of New York City's slums and tenements. The troops had made a three-week journey through rough seas in an open scow and were in deplorable physical condition. Major Arnold directed them to remove and burn their Zouave garments and replaced these with regulation army uniforms. Wilson's troops took an immediate dislike to both the regular army and regular army discipline. They went to nearly any length to make that fact evident and to irritate the regulars. A later observer reported: "Arnold tamed these men into a body of docile and well-drilled soldiers."[63]

The Zouaves, whose two companies numbered 160 soldiers, more than made up for the loss of Battery L of the First Artillery, which had been transferred to Fort Pickens on July 2. By the end of the month the strength of the garrison stood at 317. Surgeon John F. Hammond arrived on May 27 to replace Assistant Surgeon Clinton Wagner, who was reassigned to the nation's capital on July 9. As the summer heat increased, the number of soldiers hospitalized or listed as sick in quarters grew to twenty-four by the end of July. The majority of the sick were from the New York volunteers.[64]

The two companies of the Sixth New York at Fort Jefferson were much more fortunate than the remainder of their unit. In September 1861, Major Arnold was transferred and assumed command of Fort Pickens. The other seven companies of Wilson's Zouaves were stationed at that post on Santa Rosa Island, just across the bay from Pensacola. The regiment was attacked by a superior force of fifteen hundred Rebels on the dark night of October 9, 1861, while about a mile outside the walls of Fort Pickens at Camp Brown. Due to poor training and a lack of discipline on the part of the New York volunteers, the Rebels were able to destroy and burn the camp before it could be relieved by troops from the garrison.[65]

The results of the Confederate raid on Fort Pickens and Camp Brown were reported in the October 1861 monthly returns of the Department of Florida. Colonel Bill Wilson's Zouaves lost ten killed, nine wounded, and thirteen enlisted men as prisoners of war. The relief force from Fort Pickens reported four killed, twenty wounded, and one officer and eight enlisted men captured by the enemy. In defense of the Sixth New York, it should be pointed out that they were seriously outnumbered. Of 370 soldiers assigned, only 257 were present when the attack came.[66]

September 1861 was notable not only for the transfer of Major Lewis Arnold, Fort Jefferson's first wartime commander; it was also the first month that soldiers sentenced by courts-martial to confinement and hard labor made their appearance as replacements for the diminishing numbers of slaves and white civilian laborers. During the course of the war the Dry Tortugas would become the destination for hundreds of U.S. military convicts. The first fifty-three such prisoners arrived and were placed under the supervision of the commandant, the superintending engineer, and the civilian construction foreman or overseer.[67] The initial prisoners were soldiers from the 13th and 79th New York Volunteer Infantry and had been convicted of mutinous conduct. They arrived on September 4.[68]

Later the number of prisoners was significantly increased when President Lincoln eliminated the death penalty for desertion and substituted "imprisonment in the Dry Tortugas."[69] The combination of ongoing construction, civilian workers, an active military garrison, and convicts almost guaranteed that no subsequent commandant could manage the installation with any degree of order or efficiency. The three missions were in constant conflict. Both construction and the supervision of convicts interfered with the defensive posture of the fort. The nearly constant arrival of bricks and other construction materials diverted military manpower and required prisoners to be permitted outside the defensive walls, encouraging attempts at escape, which were frequent and often successful. Both soldiers and prisoners stole wood and other construction materials to improve the comfort of their quarters.

Major Arnold and his Battery C of the Second Artillery departed for Fort Pickens on September 9. Arnold was replaced as post commandant by Brevet Lieutenant Colonel Horace Brooks, the executive officer of the Second Artillery. To replace Arnold's artillerymen, Company H of the First U.S. Infantry was transferred to Fort Jefferson from Key West Barracks on September 11. The regular army company from Key West was replaced by Company A of Wilson's Zouaves, who landed briefly in the Tortugas before proceeding to Fort Taylor. Colonel Brooks brought an ordnance officer with him from Pensacola, First Lieutenant John W. Todd, to inspect the fort's armaments and ammunition storage facilities. In spite of the numerous changes, the personnel strength was virtually unchanged at the end of September with three hundred assigned.[70]

One of the standing orders current at Fort Jefferson stated that any soldier found to be drunk would be tied up in the guardhouse until sober. While neither the sutler nor the commissary would sell spirits to the enlisted soldiers, some of the engineer workmen and fishermen would. One evening a ship arrived with commissary stores, and a number of Wilson's Zouaves were tasked with their unloading. The cargo included several barrels of whiskey, some of which was consumed during the process of securing it in the storeroom. One of the New York soldiers was obviously intoxicated when the soldiers reentered the fort, and he was arrested by the guard and tied to a scaffold outside the guardhouse. As darkness fell, two large groups of Zouaves emerged from their quarters, one raiding the commissary and the other overpowering the guards and freeing their drunken companion. One sentinel fired a shot, which failed to discourage those plundering the stores, and there arose "a great uproar, a call for the guard, screaming, shouting and running from all parts of the fort toward the guardhouse."

As the confusion spread, soldiers of Company M of the regulars were ordered to arm themselves and load, and emerged running from their quarters to take up positions at the guardhouse opposite the casemates where the Zouaves were housed. A field gun was quickly added to the force attempting to restore order. The New Yorkers, soon fortified with generous quantities of whiskey, barricaded themselves in their billets and defied anyone to interfere with them. The clatter of muskets being loaded made clear their intention to defend their position. Shouted negotiations by Captain Langdon, the commander of the artillerymen, produced no results, and the mutineers refused to come out or to surrender their arms.

It was left to the garrison commander, Lieutenant Colonel Brooks, to calm the situation. A slight, small man, he remained calm and seemingly fearless as he laid aside his sword and pistol and walked directly into the Zouaves' quarters. After a good deal of loud talk and bluster, the mutineers, evidently somewhat awed by the little colonel, were pacified, and Colonel Brooks reemerged. Company M remained on guard the remainder of the night, and the New Yorkers quietly surrendered and stacked their arms as the sun rose. An investigation was then made to determine whose rifles had been loaded, and those men were later arrested when they came to reclaim their weapons. Three ringleaders were identified, charged with the insurrection, and remained imprisoned until the volunteers were transferred to join their regiment at Fort Pickens.[71]

Lieutenant Colonel Brooks received his promotion to that rank in November with an effective date of October 26, 1861. That was probably little consolation for the constant problems caused by his two companies of Wilson's Zouaves. One commander, Captain Abram T. Whiting of Company B, had been under arrest in quarters since September 23. The commander of Company E, Captain Henry DuFraine, had overstayed his leave and was listed as AWOL. Emily Holder commented that they "were without doubt very questionable characters; and, as the officers had been chosen from among themselves, the matter of discipline had been so far rather a surprise to us." November ended with twelve of the Sixth New York Volunteers in confinement for various offenses. The fifty-four soldiers from the 13th and 79th New York Regiments had been pardoned. The personnel report for the month listed them as "attached to Fort Jefferson, Fla., awaiting an opportunity to join their Regiments."[72]

The year 1861 ended quietly in the Keys and the Department of Florida. Colonel Harvey Brown received a congratulatory letter from the War Department. "The brilliant and successful operations detailed in these dispatches have been read with lively satisfaction by the President, Secretary of War, and General-in-Chief. The General will not forget to bring specially to notice the valuable services thus rendered by yourself, your officers, and your whole command, and to urge an appropriate recognition of them by the Government."[73] Colonel Brown's command included a new regiment, the 75th New York Volunteers, who were "industriously engaged in drilling." The Sixth New York, Bill Wilson's Zouaves, was evidently still a fractious and troublesome unit. Brown reported: "I am sorry to say, as far as the officers are concerned, [the regiment] is in a state of disorganization; criminations, recriminations, charges, and countercharges, between the officers, and especially between the colonel and two or three espousing his side and the other officers of the regiment, became of such daily occurrence, that I had peremptorily to stop it . . . the good of the service requires some stringent action in reference to the officers of this regiment."[74]

December was marked by further problems with prisoners at Fort Jefferson. On December 19 the U.S.S. *Rhode Island* dropped off "a U.S. marine prisoner . . . history not known." The fifty-four prisoners of the New York volunteer regiments, now pardoned, still had not been provided transportation to return to their units. Quite likely due to complaints to Colonel Brown by the commander of Fort Taylor, Company A of the Zouaves was reassigned to the Tortugas, and Company H of the First Infantry received orders to return to Key West. The transfer was completed on December 20. As the month ended, one problem was resolved. Captain Abram Whiting, former commander of the Zouaves' Company B, under arrest since September, was discharged for the good of the service effective December 25, 1861.[75]

The construction at Garden Key was well funded for the coming year. An original congressional appropriation of $65,000 had been increased by $100,000 by the secretary of war when funds for fortifications then in the hands of the Confederacy were reallocated.[76] The Thirty-Seventh Congress appropriated an additional $100,000 in June for fiscal year 1862.[77] The construction of fortifications on Bush and Bird keys was discontinued toward the end of the year. Relative quiet in the international arena as well as increased manning and armaments at Fort Jefferson had reduced feelings of insecurity that justified continued expenditure of effort and funds.

Bad Rations and Boredom in Paradise

1862

The blockade of the South declared by President Lincoln on April 19, 1861, became more effective as the war went on. Stations for vessels assigned to the Gulf Blockading Squadron were announced on January 23, 1862, and ranged all the way from Key West to the Rio Grande River in Texas. Throughout the remainder of the war Fort Jefferson and the Tortugas played a minor role in the blockade. Union steamers occasionally took on coal or emergency supplies of water at Garden Key, but nearby Key West was better stocked and served as the home port of the blockade's flagship. The Tortugas were also avoided by the blockade runners due to the high volume of federal shipping in the Florida Straits. In late January the U.S.S. *Chambers* was assigned to cruise between the Tortugas and Apalachicola, Florida.[1]

Following his promotion to brigadier general of volunteers on September 28, 1861, General John Milton Brannan assumed command of the newly organized Department of Key West on January 11, 1862.[2] A graduate of the U.S. Military Academy, Brannan had been promoted to captain of artillery in recognition of his bravery in action during the Mexican War. In early 1862 he formed a new brigade to garrison Fort Taylor, Fort Pickens, and Fort Jefferson. The brigade consisted of the Seventh New Hampshire, the 47thPennsylvania, and the 90th and 91st New York Volunteer Infantry.[3] From March 1862 through January 1864 those units provided forces to man the posts at Key West, Pensacola, and the Dry Tortugas. The northern soldiers were slow to become acclimated to the tropical climate of the department. No changes were made either to their heavy wool uniforms or to their diet, which was high in salt pork and preserved beef. Deaths from heat stroke and from fevers caused by infectious and contagious diseases were not uncommon. Officers and other leaders were insensitive to the dangers of heat injuries and often made poor decisions that exposed soldiers to unnecessary risks.

At Fort Jefferson during January 1862, the resignation of Captain Henry DuFraine of the Sixth New York Volunteers became effective on the third. Another Zouave officer, Second Lieutenant Virginius Vangeison of Company B, was placed under arrest and confined to his quarters for an unspecified offense. One of the fifty-four former prisoners of the 13th New York Volunteers, Private Columbia Page of Company H, died of disease on January 30 while the group continued to wait for a ship to return them to their regiment. Twenty-six finally departed in February, and the remainder in early March, leaving a single prisoner at the post, Marine Private William Toombs, whose offense remains a mystery.[4]

The garrison at Fort Jefferson was strengthened on March 2, 1862, by the arrival of four companies of the Seventh New Hampshire Volunteer Infantry aboard the bark *Tycoon*. In a letter to his wife Augusta, Sergeant Calvin Shedd of Company C related that the journey from the port of New York had taken seventeen days. Although he had been spared the inconvenience of seasickness, he had suffered from lack of sleep. His cold and sore throat had been cured by the warmth of the tropics, but he complained of an infection in his finger and "humors which have broken out all over me which make me itch badly." The difficulties of the voyage had been compounded by water that stank "worse than a hog pen," beef so heavily salted that it was inedible, hardtack, and "a pint of the meanest coffee" a day. As the ship lay at anchor a half mile offshore it was circled by numerous large sharks. Sergeant Shedd believed they were attracted by the corpse of a soldier of his company who had died just as they arrived at the island. That had been the second death during the trip, the first having been a man from Company G, buried at sea, who died a few days out of New York.[5]

The two surgeons on board the *Tycoon*, Dr. W. W. Brown and Assistant Surgeon Henry Boynton, were unaware of the fact that the deaths were due to smallpox. There is little doubt that had they correctly diagnosed the disease, a panic would have followed. As it was, the crew of the vessel and the four hundred soldiers quartered below decks had potentially been exposed. A tent was set up on the parade ground as a hospital and soon proved inadequate for the number of sick in the regiment. The tent quickly overflowed, and seeing the crowding, Dr. Holder of the engineers offered half the spare beds in his facility outside the fort. Dr. Brown believed that the volunteers were mainly suffering from colds and undiagnosed fevers. Later

Dr. Holder passed through the ward and noticed on one of the soldiers skin eruptions that concerned him. In consultation with the regimental surgeon, the disease was then diagnosed correctly as smallpox. A minor panic ensued although the outbreak fortunately remained limited to the New Hampshire volunteers.[6]

Ten days after the unit came ashore, the troops were ordered to be vaccinated. A quarantine hospital was soon established on nearby Bird Key for any soldiers who displayed symptoms of the disease. Three days after the doctors administered the inoculations Sergeant Shedd wrote to tell his family that "15 men have been removed to Bird Island supposed to be sick with it."[7] The eruption of festering "humors" that Shedd described was typical of a light case of smallpox in an individual who had been inoculated years before. Such cases were still highly contagious. In all about forty cases were treated and nine soldiers died.

The remaining six companies of the Seventh New Hampshire as well as their commander, Colonel Haldimand Sumner Putnam, arrived on March 9. Colonel Putnam was a native of Cornish, New Hampshire, in the western part of the state near the Connecticut River. He was accepted by the U.S. Military Academy at the age of sixteen and was commissioned in 1857 after graduating eighth in his class. Putnam served with the regular army in a variety of assignments on the western frontier. The outbreak of the Civil War found him stationed in Washington as a first lieutenant. In October 1861 he was selected by the governor of New Hampshire to command the Seventh Regiment. Following its service at Key West and the Tortugas the regiment was transferred to South Carolina, where, in July 1863, Colonel Putnam was killed in action storming the ramparts of Fort Wagner. Although a strict and demanding commander, he was held in the highest regard by his officers and soldiers.[8]

Their ship, the clipper *S.R. Mallory*, was delayed by a lack of favorable winds. Because of the delays, water had to be rationed, and several soldiers were apprehended stealing from the ship's stores and water casks. They were later brought before a court-martial at Fort Jefferson and were sentenced to confinement and the indignity of wearing a ball and chain. Upon arrival, the ship ran aground on a sandbar just off Garden Key, and the soldiers had to be shuttled to the fort in a small steamer, the *Union*, which happened to be in port. Colonel Putnam assumed command of the garrison on March 12, 1862, relieving Lieutenant Colonel Brooks. Brooks returned to Fort Pickens and his unit with regular army surgeon J. F. Hammond. The New Hampshire Volunteers were the largest unit ever to man the post, having 950 assigned, and the three companies of Zouaves were released to return to their regiment. Sergeant Calvin Shedd commented: "We expect they will go to Santa Rosa Island soon God speed them for they are an awfull hard set."[9] They sailed to join their regiment at Fort Pickens, grateful, no doubt, to have left before the smallpox outbreak became more widespread.[10] Battery M of the First U.S. Artillery remained to man the guns and train the soldiers of the Seventh New Hampshire on artillery drills.

The addition of a full regiment to the garrison far exceeded the number of completed quarters available, and orderly rows of tents sprang up both inside and outside the walls of the fort. Emily Holder wrote: "The parade was quickly converted into an impromptu camp-ground; tents were pitched, guns stacked, and, as if by magic, camp fires appeared with men sitting around eating, their knapsacks serving as tables, or reading the letters they found awaiting them. All were evidently delighted to be on shore even though the island was not larger than one of their fields at home in New Hampshire." The soldiers soon found, however, that their tropical paradise was to be shared with a large population of biting insects as well as small scorpions that found knapsacks, bedrolls, and boxes a welcome refuge from the sun.[11]

The lighthouse keeper, a Mr. Brannan (no relation to the general), had two slaves, a girl of about twenty and a boy of fifteen, "keen as a briar" in Sergeant Shedd's opinion. When Wilson's Zouaves left Garden Key, the young man stowed away and went with them to Pensacola. Brannan soon figured out where the boy had gone and had him returned. The post had a regulation that no one could be punished without the permission of the garrison commander. With this in mind, the lighthouse keeper went to see Colonel Putnam in his office. The colonel listened patiently to the old man's explanation of why the boy well deserved to be whipped for his offense. When Brannan concluded, Colonel Putnam looked at him seriously and said with clarity, "You go to Hell," and returned to his work. It was evident that the institution of slavery had few sympathizers in New Hampshire.[12]

A second example of the difficulties the New Englanders had with the treatment of slaves was reported by overseer George Phillips to Lieutenant McFarland on May 28, 1862. The New Hampshire soldiers sometimes encouraged the slaves to resist degrading authority. In one incident a slave named Mingo defied Phillips's orders, believing he would be "backed up" by his new Yankee acquaintances. The overseer imprisoned Mingo in one of the unused powder magazines to await a change in his insubordinate attitude. Some time later when Phillips was bringing the prisoner his meal, a

Figure 12. Original 1826 Garden Key light and unfinished enlisted men's barracks in 1864. Courtesy National Archives, 77F74-79A.

few of the soldiers threatened Phillips with their weapons, shouting: "Lock him up! Put him in and see how *he* likes it." Phillips quickly lodged a protest with Colonel Putnam, and the matter was put to rest. The slave remained in confinement until he became more compliant.[13]

The need for laborers to complete the officers' quarters and barracks and to complete the third tier of the curtain walls was critical; the number of slaves available for hire on Key West was limited, and white labor was in short supply. On March 29, 1862, the adjutant general informed Major General D. Hunter, commander of the Department of the South, that Brigadier General Brannan "has requested that 200 contrabands be sent from Port Royal [South Carolina] for the public works at Fort Jefferson, Tortugas. The Secretary of War directs that they be sent accordingly."[14] *Contrabands* was the military term for escaped slaves who had succeeded in passing through Union lines. They complicated operations for commanders by creating an increased demand for rations as well as crowding areas behind the front lines with what amounted to a population of refugees. Some able-bodied male contrabands became teamsters or laborers for the federal forces. Later many enlisted in the Union Army. The laborers transported to Fort Jefferson would have been paid $1.12 a day and would have been provided quarters, rations, and medical support. Department commanders were required to report the "number, age, and condition of the Africans who have been under your supervision while in your present command, with the amount of work performed by them, the pay received, and the cost to the Government for their support."[15] There is no evidence that the requested contrabands were ever sent to the Tortugas. The engineers' "slave roll" contains the only record of black workers through the summer of 1863.

Among the construction workers encountered at Fort Jefferson by the New Hampshire regiment were the twenty or so slaves and their families from Key West. Calvin Shedd related seeing many of them, men, women, and children. "They were the first slaves I ever saw I have not talked with any of them yet they appear to be pretty well contented on the outside all I know about them is they are awfull Black." One of the soldiers soon organized a school of sorts for the slaves. Shedd wrote to his wife: "Shaker is busy Sundays & evenings teaching the slaves to read they are extremely pleased when they can spell words of three letters they astonish themselves in the progress they make. The Boys plague Shaker about his Niggers and ask him what he reads to them he answered the other night when asked the question By G-d, I read the Bible to them Shaker is a Brick we have a great deal of fun with him."[16]

April of 1862 witnessed an event that seemed to prove that the brick and mortar fortifications of the Third System, Fort Jefferson among them, had

Figure 13. Dismounted 30-pounder Parrott rifle on barbette atop east curtain 2. Photo by Paulien Reid.

become obsolete. The event was an attack on Confederate-held Fort Pulaski at the mouth of the Savannah River in Georgia. Construction of the fort had begun in 1829 and had been completed in 1847. In terms of its architecture it was identical to the fort on Garden Key in both engineering and structure; the greatest difference between them was that Fort Pulaski had only one level of casemates rather than the two tiers found at Fort Jefferson. General David Hunter, commander of the Department of the South, ordered a bombardment of Fort Pulaski on April 10, 1862, and requested assistance from Commander C. R. P. Rodgers of the U.S. Navy Flagship *Wabash*, who had a number of experienced gunners.[17]

Commander Rogers later described the attack in a letter to his superior, Admiral S. F. DuPont:

> On the second day, in spite of a high wind, the firing from the rifled guns [30–pounder Parrott rifles] and columbiads was excellent, the former boring into the brick face of the wall like augers, the latter striking like trip hammers and breaking off great masses of masonry which had been cut loose by the rifles.
>
> The four upper batteries [on Tybee Island] were above 1,600 yards distant from Pulaski, and quite beyond the distance at which it has hitherto been held practicable to effect a breach, but which proved an easy breaching range with these wonderful projectiles which we now possess.
>
> When the fort surrendered, the barbette guns had been silenced and many of them had been dismounted; the breach was practicable in two places, and could have been stormed without doubt. Our projectiles were passing through it and were knocking down the opposite wall, which protected the main magazine, so that the garrison was convinced that in an hour or two the magazine must be blown up.[18]

The Confederate garrison of Fort Pulaski surrendered at 2:00 p.m. on April 11, 1862.

Did the fate of Fort Pulaski prove that Third System fortifications like Fort Jefferson were no longer viable? At least one recent author believes it did not. He points out that the Confederates were equipped with inferior guns, the range of which was far shorter than that of the more modern weapons emplaced on Tybee Island. It was only this disparity in range that allowed Union gunners to hammer away at the walls without the fear and disruption of counterbattery fire from the fort. Had the armaments been equal, the fate of Fort Pulaski might have been quite different.[19]

Even before the attack on Fort Pulaski it was evident that the engineer and ordnance departments were raising the standard for arming coastal fortifications. On April 2, 1862, Sergeant Shedd commented on Fort Jefferson's increasingly modern armaments. "There was 6 [84-pounder] rifled Cannon arrived here the other day they are to be mounted on top of the walls." Less than a year later the department commander, General David Hunter, encouraged the general-in-chief that Garden Key "should be armed to [its] utmost capacity with a large proportion of guns of the heaviest caliber known."[20]

The number of military convicts at Fort Jefferson during the spring and summer of 1862 was negligible. Letters and other materials from the months that the Seventh New Hampshire manned the garrison make no mention of them. This is illustrated by the estimate of the post's population at about fifteen hundred. The New Hampshire contingent numbered nearly one thousand, the departing Zouaves totaled three hundred, and the remainder consisted of the regular army artillerymen and the engineer workmen and slaves. The only prisoner listed on the March personnel return was Marine William Toombs. There were no convicts in close confinement; Calvin Shedd reported on March 15 that the Zouaves had departed, and "the Guard House is to let this morning."[21]

Sergeant Shedd wrote to his wife on March 24: "Men are dying at the rate of one a day of small Pox. L[evi] L. Page of my squad is dead of it and his Brother Corporal [John] Page is very sick." Two days later he reported that "two more of our men, Mr. [Charles F.] Sprague & [William P.] Hardy died one yesterday the other today of Small Pox we hope that will be all." On April 2 he wrote of a final casualty, "Copl. [John] C. Page died last night of small pox, which makes three out of my squad. I hope it is the last the Doctr thinks there will be no more cases; there has been 9 deaths from it in the regt 4 of Co C—5 of Co G." The healthy soldiers were doing their best to take advantage of the post's limited recreations. "Some of the Boys went out in a boat yesterday and Harpooned a Shark and brought him ashore he was about 8 ft long an ugly looking customer."[22]

The garrison drew their rations from depot stocks stored there, the majority of which had exceeded their shelf life. The tropical climate encouraged decay and the proliferation of weevils and other insects. On April 2 Sergeant Shedd noted, "Our Grub will make us all sick I am afraid the Coffee stinks so that no one but a Soldier could drink it or the Tea either; our bread is all made of damaged Flour." The water in the subterranean cisterns had been contaminated by mosquitoes, which laid eggs that emerged after a few days as very active larvae. The men treated it as a matter of course. "I have just been to dinner we had boiled Pork Potatoes & a piece of Bread & a dish of Rain water with wiggles in it we drink lots of wiggles & the bread is filled with Black Bugs about 1/4 of an inch long we pick out some of them & eat the rest there is scarcly anything that turns my stomach now it has got to be proof against dirt & nastiness."[23]

It is striking that Dr. Holder, the engineer physician, or Seventh New Hampshire Surgeon W. W. Brown did not condemn the rations in storage and encourage their disposal somewhere offshore. Even the hardtack, usually a nearly indestructible commodity, had become infested. "We had boiled Mutton & Broth with Hard-Bread for dinner the best dinner we have had for 2 weeks notwithstanding worms & inch long that came out of the Bread [and] were crawling off the table yesterday there was one full an inch long on my plate I poked him off, and continued my dinner."[24] Not surprisingly, the hospital treated a continuous stream of soldiers complaining of intestinal problems. Reports listed 106 sick in April and 142 in May, many from dysentery.[25]

Unlike their Zouave volunteer predecessors at Garden Key, the New Hampshire regiment took drill and training seriously and made steady improvement. They were quite critical of officers who did not demonstrate equal dedication to the task and achieve similar progress. The men of the Seventh also took full advantage of the expertise of the regular army artillerymen and mastered drills on the fort's heavy guns. Colonel Putnam used the time the unit had at Fort Jefferson to prepare the men for combat and to eliminate those who could not measure up to standard, often because of age or physical disability.

Despite the often discussed labor shortage, construction continued through the spring and summer of 1862 under the supervision of the civilian supervisors. Engineer Captain James Morton had departed on March 15, shortly after the Seventh arrived. After nearly a year in the Tortugas, his health had declined to such an extent that Dr. Whitehurst, the post's civilian physician, recommended he spend several months in the north to recover.[26] Unlike later commandants, Colonel Putnam seems to have had no complaints or disagreements with the engineers. Having few other interesting topics to discuss in his letters to his family, Sergeant Shedd included notes on the progress of the builders. "They have gained some on the Fort since we came they are now building the magazines on the Parapet. Brick arrive here in large quantities they cost the Government $17.00 per M & come from Maine. They have got the new Condencer at work and it makes much better water than we have had heretofore. It is very clear and tastes much better than that made by the old one."[27] The two steam condensers had been ordered from New York by Colonel Putnam and were capable of distilling seven thousand gallons of sea water a day. They were used throughout the war. The water was stored in cisterns separate from those used for rainwater catchment but also located beneath the parade ground.[28]

In addition to the magazines on the upper level mentioned by Sergeant Shedd, the masons had made progress on the barbette tier flooring, the stairway towers, the cornice of the parade field, and the stairways to the shot cellars. A furnace to heat solid projectiles had been completed on the parade ground. A considerable effort had been made to repair and maintain temporary frame buildings, still in use after nearly twenty years. The carpenters also built a small flat barge to transport sand and coral stone from the nearby keys. The barge probably replaced the one borrowed and lost at sea by Colonel Harvey Brown's expedition in April of the previous year.[29]

The strength of the garrison was considerably reduced following the departure of the Seventh New Hampshire on June 16. Colonel Putnam relinquished command of the post to Lieutenant Colonel Louis W. Tinelli, battalion commander of four companies of the 90th New York Volunteer Infantry. The soldiers of the Seventh boarded the same vessel that had brought the 90th from Key West. At the end of the month, Tinelli reported with evident irritation the condition in which he found the headquarters. He noted that "125 men were left behind on the sick list or awaiting their discharge all of their accoutrements and even part of their equipments were carried away by the commanders of their respective companies: no descriptive lists, no rolls left, no blanks books, stamps or stationery was left at the Post: Even the Hospital Record was carried away by the Regts Doctor." The monthly return for June was not on the printed government form but was prepared on several pieces of lined notebook paper pasted together to achieve the necessary length.[30]

For an officer in the American Civil War, Colonel Louis W. Tinelli had a very unusual background. The scion of a powerful family of the Austrian nobility, he was commissioned and served in northern Italy. He became involved with liberal elements and as a result lost his commission and was banished. His political activities also became known in Piedmont, where King Charles Felix had him imprisoned for over three years. When Charles Albert ascended the throne in 1831 he lifted the threatened death penalty for nine political prisoners, including Tinelli, but banished them from the kingdom. Tinelli then traveled to the United States, where he established himself in New York City and secured American citizenship. There he was close friends with the future French king Napoleon III (nephew of the emperor), who had also been expelled from his native country. Tinelli's broad understanding of European affairs brought him to the attention of the U.S. Department of State, and he was appointed consul to Oporto. He served in Portugal until 1850. At the time of the outbreak of the Civil War he was consul to Palermo.

Tinelli resigned his post in the summer of 1861 and returned to New York. He recruited a volunteer unit, the McClellan Chasseurs, in November and December 1861. That unit was eventually consolidated with another volunteer battalion, the McClellan Rifles, and formed the 90th New York Volunteer Infantry commanded by Colonel Joseph Morgan. Tinelli was elected to the second post, that of lieutenant colonel. The regiment was deployed to Key West on January 5, 1862, where it was attached to General Brannan's Florida Expedition.[31]

As of July 31, 1862, the Department of the South reported only thirteen officers and 222 enlisted soldiers present for duty out of a total assigned of 283. The difference indicated that forty-eight soldiers were sick in quarters, hospitalized, or in confinement.[32] An epidemic of yellow fever broke out at Key West in the latter part of July. Captain Morton's replacement as superintending engineer of Forts Taylor and Jefferson, First Lieutenant Walter McFarland, later reported that two engineer employees died there on July 28 and that he had been hospitalized on July 30. The outbreak killed twenty-eight civilian workers, and eight remained bedridden as of the first week of September.[33] At Fort Jefferson, Company M, First U.S. Artillery, was transferred during July, but the personnel return fails to mention a date, destination, or order number. During August four soldiers joined Marine Private William Toombs on the listing of prisoners: Privates Patrick Carroll and Thomas Carlton of the 47th New York Volunteers and John Fakey and Fred Smith of the Sixth Connecticut Volunteers were sentenced to the Tortugas by court-martial. Of the soldiers left behind by the Seventh New Hampshire, thirty-seven regained their health and were sent to Hilton Head, South Carolina, to rejoin their regiment. The remainder were discharged and sent home with the exception of two soldiers still hospitalized at the end of August. The heat of late summer also had an impact on the soldiers of the 90th New York. Fifteen became ill that month, and four died.[34]

At Key West the 90th New York's commander, Colonel Joseph Morgan, evidently an abolitionist and perhaps anticipating the later actions of his commander in chief, decided to declare the slaves employed at Fort Taylor and Fort Jefferson to be free of their owners. Lieutenant Walter McFarland, the superintending engineer at Key West, protested Morgan's action, and the slaves responded by abandoning the job site. Colonel Morgan offered to order them to return to work if McFarland would pay them regular workers' wages. McFarland refused, not only because of the legal problems it would have caused with the slaves' owners but because lack of funds had caused even his white workers to be four months behind in their wages.[35] The problem was eventually resolved by a return to the status quo.

Along with recovered soldiers sent to rejoin the regiment, a number of other soldiers of the Seventh New Hampshire who had been too ill to move earlier were among those who left Fort Jefferson in August. Dr. C. H. Crane, medical director of the Department of the South, reported: "They were all men who had been invalids for a long time and broken down in constitution." The soldiers left for Hilton Head, South Carolina, aboard the steamer *Delaware* about August 11, 1862. The ship arrived on August 26 and was quarantined for twelve days before the passengers were permitted to disembark. At the end of quarantine Surgeon J. C. Dalton, a passenger on the vessel, reported that no one aboard was ill. In spite of that precaution, nine of the New Hampshire volunteers began to exhibit symptoms of yellow fever three days after landing. By September 19, eight of the men had died of the infection. Strangely, no other soldiers aboard the *Delaware* showed any sign of the disease.[36]

The last few months the 90th New York volunteers were stationed at Fort Jefferson were marked by the highest mortality the post had seen. Fatalities from August through October were eleven enlisted soldiers and one officer, First Lieutenant William R. Hill. During the four months ending in December 1862, ninety-one soldiers or 35 percent of the unit had been reported hospitalized.[37] Marine Private William Toombs was released by order of the secretary of the navy and departed on September 8, leaving only four prisoners still incarcerated. The second battalion of the 47th Pennsylvania Volunteer Infantry arrived at the Tortugas on Sunday, December 21, 1862, aboard the steamship *Cosmopolitan* and relieved the battalion of the 90th New York, which returned to Key West on December 22.[38]

In accordance with Special Order 384, Department of the South, Lieutenant Colonel George W. Alexander took command of the post upon arrival. One soldier wrote that the 90th New York had suffered nearly 50 percent casualties from a yellow fever outbreak at Key West, describing the disease as "more deadly than the bullot."

Colonel Good, the 47th Pennsylvania's regimental commander, had received orders from General Brannan on December 16, 1862, stressing the importance of Forts Taylor and Jefferson. "It is hardly necessary to point out to you the extreme military importance of the two works now entrusted to your command. . . . In view of difficulties that may soon culminate in war with foreign powers, it is eminently necessary that these works should be immediately placed beyond any possibility of seizure."[39]

The officers and soldiers of the 47th Pennsylvania fell into the same routines that had been pursued by their predecessors—guard duty, inspections, fishing, shell collecting, and hunting turtles and bird eggs.. Lieutenant Breneman of Company H noted that there were six families living there, including twelve or so "respectable ladies." He also reported that the officers' quarters had several large rooms that were regularly used for balls and parties.[40]

The giant sea turtles that had given the islands their name returned each year to lay eggs in the sand of their places of origin. The meat of the turtles was prized as a welcome change from salt pork and beef, but the turtle eggs were eaten only by "negroes and soldiers." Emily Holder, the wife of engineer surgeon Joseph Holder, described an outing on nearby Loggerhead Key: "We took three boats, with music for dancing and supper, making a grand frolic of the occasion. After supper, enjoyed in the lighthouse living room, the ample kitchen was converted into a ballroom and dancing indulged in until it was nearly time for the turtles to come up when, taking our shawls and wraps, we started for the beach. Dividing up into parties of six we stationed ourselves like a picket along the shore, not daring to speak aloud, as the least disturbance would alarm the turtles and deter them from coming on shore."[41]

A later account by a soldier assigned to the post was more graphic.

When the monstrous turtle crawls up from the water . . . a rush is suddenly made upon him by the boys; some head him off from the water, while the rest lay violent hands on him. He is quickly turned on his back, and his feet, or flippers, are adroitly secured by a strong line. If not the next morning consigned to the tender mercies of the post butcher, a string is placed round his neck, to which is attached a small board, marked with the letter of the company to which he belongs. He is then thrown in the breakwater, or moat, that surrounds the fort, to float around in lazy indolence until the company cook intimates that his presence is needed in the kitchen.[42]

Turtles on the beaches were of course females, coming ashore only to lay eggs, but this one immediately became "him" in the soldier's account of the capture.

The larger numbers of ill soldiers and increases in deaths from disease at Fort Jefferson were not due to a lack of skilled medical staff. In addition to Dr. Holder of the engineers, the garrison had the services of Dr. Daniel Whitehurst, a civilian physician from Key West. Whitehurst had served in the Seminole Wars in Florida, attaining the rank of major in the volunteers. He had studied medicine at New York University, graduating in the 1840s. Some accounts suggest that Whitehurst, a Virginia native, resigned his position as surgeon at Fort Jefferson due to his wife's sympathies for the southern cause, but evidence showed that he was still performing his duties there as late as September 1862.[43] Following the stationing of the 47th Pennsylvania in December, personnel returns also list Dr. Jacob H. Sheetz as the post's assistant surgeon.[44] Rather, the high number of fatalities is probably attributable to poor nutrition and tropical disease, neither of which was understood with any certainty by nineteenth-century medicine.

As 1862 came to a close, the number of U.S. warships in the waters off the Florida reef made it clear that the naval blockade of the Confederacy was gaining in effectiveness. In the east, General McClellan's failure to achieve his objectives in northern Virginia and the devastating level of casualties at Antietam in September led President Lincoln to relieve McClellan of command. In the west General Grant had significant victories at Fort Henry and Donelson and had won at Shiloh at great cost. The fall of New Orleans to Union forces was cheering, but Vicksburg and Port Hudson still effectively blocked the Mississippi. It was clear the struggle would be a long one.

Construction, Convicts, and the Pennsylvania Volunteers

1863

At the beginning of 1863 Fort Jefferson still faced a threat from Confederate attack, however small. During the tenure of the 47th Pennsylvania Veteran Volunteers that year, the post's population of military convicts was not significant. In January only three prisoners remained in custody. The population peaked in November with 214 incarcerated. At that level, the demands of the engineers for unskilled construction labor could be met and managed with efficiency. For most of the year, the ratio of soldiers to prisoners was about four to one. Following the Union victories at Vicksburg and Gettysburg in July 1863, however, a belief that the Confederacy posed a serious threat to the fortress in the Tortugas was no longer credible. As the strategic value of Fort Jefferson declined, its use as a dumping ground for the victims of military justice increased. Policy changes by the Lincoln administration the next year eliminated execution as a punishment for desertion and substituted hard labor in the Tortugas. Declining emphasis on the defense of the installation is indicated by the removal of two companies of the garrison to the regiment's headquarters at Key West, one in May and a second in October 1863.

The depressed level of personnel manning the garrison continued throughout the winter of 1862–63. Early in the year the situation was seen as serious, and General Hunter, commanding the Department of the South, referred to it in a letter to Henry W. Halleck, the general-in-chief of the army, on February 24, 1863. Hunter reported that the garrison of the Tortugas was only two hundred men of the thousand required; he suggested that an additional volunteer regiment should be raised for that specific purpose with "men, if possible, to some extent acclimated and under officers with some artillery experience." He added that "regiments of blacks might find proper service here" and that command "could be given to an old artillery officer with the necessary rank ... perhaps incapable of field duty elsewhere." Hunter included the information that the armament of Fort Jefferson was composed of "six 10-inch, thirty 8-inch, and nine 42-pounder guns, and six 84-pounders, rifled; total, 51 guns." He concluded with a recommendation that Key West and the Tortugas should be armed to the fullest extent possible with "guns of the heaviest caliber known" and that both installations were dangerously vulnerable to Confederate attack.[1] General Hunter's concerns were the last to be expressed concerning the forts in the Florida Keys during the remainder of the war.

The routine of military duty during the tenure of the 47th Pennsylvania was well documented in the diaries and letters of its enlisted soldiers. The diary of Corporal George Washington Albert of Company H is particularly useful in illustrating the mind-numbing boredom of service in the Tortugas. Typical entries record time, temperature and weather, formations and inspections, tours of guard duty, and Albert's constant preoccupation with minor ailments, discomforts, and illnesses. Garden Key served as a major supply storage depot throughout the war although the tropical climate made it a poor environment for holding perishable rations. Corporal Albert noted on January 20, 1863, that a sailing ship "came from Orleanes for a load of old pork and flower wich is nearly spoilt, there is thousands of barrels here not fit for use."[2] Later descriptions of the rations prepared for the soldiers and prisoners indicated that they were drawing their supplies from the same source. In 1860 Emily Holder had observed: "The flour grew poor, the weevils shared it with us; we could see them flying in the air near the casemate where a quantity of flour was stored."[3]

News of Lincoln's Emancipation Proclamation issued on January 1, 1863, arrived at Key West about January 9 and somewhat later at the Tortugas. Although the declaration applied only to slaves in areas "in rebellion," a more liberal interpretation was evidently enforced by Colonel Morgan of the 90th New York, temporarily commanding Key West. The engineers' senior officer, Captain McFarland, however, continued to direct payments for black workers at Key West and Garden Key to their owners rather than to the workers. The slave roll at Fort Jefferson was maintained until June 18, 1863, for the twenty-two blacks employed there. Finally, pressure from Washington convinced McFarland to begin paying his workers directly. Free black workers from Key West continued to refuse to work at the Tortugas regardless of what wages were offered. The War Department tried to make up the shortfall by sending one hundred freed blacks to Garden Key from Louisiana.[4]

The regimental commander and several companies of the 47th Pennsylvania that had spent three weeks on temporary duty in South Carolina returned to Key West on February 27, 1863. Colonel Good resumed command and discovered that Colonel Morgan of the 90th New York had issued orders deporting 730 citizens of Key West because they had relatives serving the Confederacy. These unfortunates, limited by order to fifty pounds of baggage each, were about to embark on a ship to Hilton Head, where they would be passed through the lines to the Rebels. Emily Holder commented: "Colonel Morgan . . . had been rather playing the tyrant. He had perverted a very good order of General Hunter into one that ordered every person who had friends in the rebel service to leave Key West."[5] Colonel Good immediately rescinded the orders and sent the civilians to their homes "until treason is proved against them." Colonel Joseph Morgan was directed to report to Department Headquarters and was eventually dismissed from the service on April 19, 1864. The War Department later determined that Morgan's overzealous interpretation of a general order regarding possible Confederate sympathizers did not merit his dismissal.[6] The combination of Morgan's liberation of the slaves in the summer of 1862 and his attempted deportation of a large part of Key West's peaceful civilian population left his superiors with serious questions regarding Morgan's judgment.

Due to General Hunter's earlier concerns about the personnel strength at Fort Jefferson, companies E and G of the 47th Pennsylvania were transferred there February 28, 1863, increasing the average manning to roughly 557 effective soldiers.[7] A growing number of prisoners also warranted a larger garrison. In a command realignment the District of Key West and Tortugas was transferred from General Hunter's Department of the South to Major General Nathaniel P. Banks's Department of the Gulf on March 16, 1863. Brigadier General Daniel P. Woodbury, who had directed construction at Garden Key as a lieutenant and captain, was assigned as district commander. At that time, units assigned to the district remained the 90th New York, now commanded by Lieutenant Colonel Louis W. Tinelli, and the 47th Pennsylvania under the command of Colonel Good. The total strength of the two units was 1,565 as of April 1863.[8]

After recovering from his bout with yellow fever Captain McFarland spent the winter working in the Corps of Engineers' office in New York. Although he had received permission to take his family with him to Key

West, the difficulties with securing transportation in the wartime environment caused him to change his mind. After waiting six weeks for space on a steamer he finally left New York bound for Key West on January 23, 1863, and arrived on January 30. McFarland's first duty was an unpleasant one. During his fifteen-week absence, the draftsman, a Mr. Jekyll, had been accused of drunkenness and "gross misconduct." Finding the allegations true, McFarland fired him. The agency in New York eventually found a replacement, civil engineer Edward Frost, who was hired in March 1863 for duty at Fort Jefferson.[9]

Dr. Joseph Holder, the surgeon assigned to the engineers at Fort Jefferson, commented that "the summer of 1863 was remarkably hot, and the rebellion at its height. Prisoners of all complexions were thronging the fortress, and still they came. . . . Nearly all were badly tainted with scurvy; and no more unfavorable place could be selected . . . particularly on account of the scarcity of vegetables. . . . Nearly nine hundred prisoners and a regiment of infantry were quartered within the walls of the fortress."[10] The post surgeon expressed concern at his inability to provide citrus fruit or green vegetables to cure or prevent a worsening of the scurvy, which could result in death if left untreated. Dr. Holder searched the nearby keys and found that the herb purslain grew here and there in large quantities, particularly in areas that had recently been dug up or disturbed. Boats were dispatched and "loads were brought in and distributed among the various messes. The purslain was boiled, and used as greens, with vinegar and pepper. This, of itself, was not only useful to a wonderful degree as an antiscorbutic, but it proved a luxury as an article of diet."[11] Holder's account, written five or six years after the war, is confused. He was treating scurvy in 1863, but for about 130 prisoners; the comments regarding a regiment of infantry and nine hundred convicts describe conditions in the summer of 1864.

Other opinions of the healthy herbs were less positive. Corporal Albert, then detailed as a cook, recalled that on Saturday, April 4, salt beef was served for breakfast and a "mess of parsley for dinner which did not take well." Sergeant William C. Hutcheson, the provost noncommissioned officer, took four men, probably prisoners, to Loggerhead Key in one of the small boats "to bring back vegetables for the command by order of the commanding officer." The emphasis on "command" probably indicated that Hutcheson had little enthusiasm for the mission. Other routine tasks that fell to the provost sergeant were towing out a floating target for artillery practice and hauling garbage to be dumped into the bay, including hides and entrails when animals were slaughtered for fresh meat. In military terms, collecting trash was referred to as *police call*, and rubbish in general as *police matter*. Some literal-minded officer of the Pennsylvania regiment evidently drew an inaccurate link between "police" and the duties of the provost marshal's office and wrote Sergeant Hutcheson's job description accordingly.[12]

Although the army commissary service delivered live cattle and hogs from time to time, the majority of the rations were canned, dried, or salted. Typical menus recorded by Corporal Albert during April 1863 were fresh [boiled] beef for breakfast, bean soup for dinner, and salt pork for supper. Other main courses that figured prominently and frequently were "snits and dough," fried mush, boiled mush, salt beef, canned vegetable soup with dough, rice soup, and pea soup; as a variation on salt pork for breakfast, hot pork was sometimes substituted. Albert mentioned baking four dried peach snits pies, but these he sold for twenty-five cents each rather than serving them to the soldiers. The Pennsylvania regiment was largely of German extraction, and some soldiers used the term *snits* to describe anything cut into fine pieces. One unfortunate result of the diet and the bad condition of the rations was that in March fifty-two soldiers were admitted to the hospital with "putrid diarrhea," and in an average month thirty or forty were admitted, the majority suffering from dysentery or diarrhea.[13]

On April 10 the steamship *Blackston* arrived from New York with a cargo of troops, supplies, and 105 prisoners accompanied by thirty-four guards. Using small boats, Sergeant Hutcheson supervised the unloading and transfer of the prisoners. The convicts were then turned over to the officer of the guard, Lieutenant Hunsberger.[14] Among the military prisoners delivered were a number of "bounty jumpers." These were men who had volunteered in units offering an enlistment bonus, often several hundred dollars. Once the bounty or bonus was paid they deserted their units and began a search for another regiment offering a bonus. Such men were subjected by the army to the harshest possible treatment and generally arrived at the Dry Tortugas under a life sentence of hard labor. At the end of the month, the post returns for Fort Jefferson reflected 666 soldiers present, 544 from the six companies of the 47th Pennsylvania, 115 prisoners, and seven "unassigned," presumably recruits or transients.[15]

Concerns regarding hygiene increased as temperatures rose and the population housed within the installation increased. Spring of 1863 added the overpowering odors of human waste to those of the decaying shellfish collected by the soldiers as souvenirs. The sanitary facilities of the fort were among its greatest engineering failures. During the early phases of construction, all outhouses had been located outside the walls. As the garrison grew, crude toilets were constructed on the lower level, designed to use the action of the tides to flush sewers into the surrounding moat. In theory the effluent would then be washed from the moat into the open bay, again by tidal action. By April it was clear that theory had failed. Lieutenant Colonel Alexander later ordered newly arrived engineer Edward Frost to breach the seawall or (counterscarp) at several points to facilitate drainage with the ebb and flow of the tide. Sergeant Hutcheson put twenty-seven convicts on detail cleaning the offending material out of the breakwater or moat. He reported it to be "very filthy." The problem was aggravated by soldiers disposing of garbage through the gun ports of their living areas, which were casemates converted into barracks. A few days later Hutcheson complained that the men on guard were "very dirty . . . they ease themselves of nature on the ramparts and embrasures."[16] The sergeant was not the first or last to complain about the sanitary habits of Civil War soldiers.

Relations between the engineers and Lieutenant Colonel Alexander were strained during much of the time the 47th Pennsylvania remained at Fort Jefferson. Captain McFarland, the superintending engineer for both Fort Taylor and the Tortugas, left construction at Fort Jefferson in the hands of civilian subordinates, preferring to reside at Key West. On June 26, 1863, McFarland was notified of the assignment of an assistant, Lieutenant Asa Holgate, recently graduated from the U.S. Military Academy. Holgate arrived at Key West and was immediately assigned to Fort Jefferson. Prior to Holgate's arrival, however, matters were in the hands of Edward Frost. Frost had the irritating habit of putting all complaints in the form of letters, in spite of the fact that his office was only a few hundred yards from that of the garrison commander. In a series of letters begun in May, Frost first complained about soldiers removing the wooden covers of the cisterns, located in the center of each ground floor room. Removal of the covers allowed dirt to contaminate the drinking water and, although Frost did not mention it, also allowed mosquitoes to lay their eggs, resulting in water filled with mosquito larvae or "wigglers." He pointed out that once installed, the covers were no longer the responsibility of the engineers.[17]

Frost next wrote to Alexander stating that the engineers wanted to reclaim two kitchens at the rear of the officers' quarters. Another letter protested the lack of a general order forbidding the taking of wood from job sites or storage buildings, whether "blocks, sticks, boards, barrel staves, fire wood, or any other kind.." All was "public property [and] should be prohibited to be used at all except by order of the proper officer to whose keeping it may belong." A soldier had written to his family about a year earlier: "I am writing on a new table that I have just finished of rough boards that I stole of Uncle Sam."[18] Alexander countered Frost's grousing by noting that the post surgeon had complained of the garbage and offal collecting in the breakwater and declared that it posed a threat to good hygiene. The engineers were ordered to remove the construction cofferdam on the northwest side of the fort and replace it with a floodgate that could be opened to allow the flotsam to be purged by the tide. The engineer workmen spent Wednesday, June 17, clearing "stagnant water" out of two sections of the moat.[19]

Three days later two of the prisoners, whose names were not recorded, made the first successful escape from Fort Jefferson. Unobserved by the guards the two stowed away on the bark *H. Booth* after unloading one of the innumerable loads of bricks that were shipped to the post from Maine. The ship departed on June 20. Over the next few years, this method of desertion from the Tortugas was generally the most successful. Due to the war, the draft, and nearly full employment in war industries in the North, most commercial vessels were critically short of able seamen. Few of the prisoners at Fort Jefferson were imprisoned for offenses that would have been considered serious in the civilian world. The masters of the ships employing escaped convicts as able seamen probably were taking no more risk than if they had hired men in a waterfront bar elsewhere. The escape in June was the only such desertion recorded in detail by the 47th Pennsylvania in 1863.[20]

A welcome break from the social isolation of the officers and their families on Garden Key came in July with visits from Lieutenant Commander Ralph Chandler aboard the flagship U.S.S. *San Jacinto* and Captain Edward Van Sice of the gunboat U.S.S. *Sunflower*. An exchange in hospitality was enjoyed with dinner parties aboard ship and in the ballroom of the officers' quarters. Dr. Holder's wife recalled that the visits "brought a bit of life and sunshine that was really the beginning of brighter days." The *Sunflower*, part of the newly organized East Gulf Blockading Squadron, had been assigned a patrol area just north of the Tortugas and found frequent cause to call on Fort Jefferson.[21]

One month before on June 13, 1863, Captain Van Sice had paused at Garden Key to take on coal when the ship's watch saw a suspicious schooner standing motionless to the southeast. The captain "immediately ordered steam, and as soon as the same was reported ready started the chase." The *Sunflower* quickly overtook the schooner—but not before a load of cotton bales on deck had been jettisoned to improve her speed. The vessel was the blockade runner *Pushmataha*. The admiralty court at Key West evidently was unable to establish guilt and allowed the ship to return to Havana. The *Pushmataha* had a second, fatal encounter with the U.S. Navy off Sabine Pass, Texas, on October 7, 1863. When overtaken by the gunship U.S.S. *Cayuga*, her crew abandoned ship for the Louisiana coast. The cargo proved to be rum, wine, and a large quantity of French gunpowder. After the navy had removed the cargo, the schooner was set on fire with two of the powder kegs remaining aboard to ensure its complete destruction.[22]

With few exceptions, the prisoners sentenced to the Dry Tortugas were soldiers convicted by court-martial for desertion, cowardice, mutiny, and a host of other offenses against the laws of war. Dr. Holder had a low opinion of the quality of justice dispensed in many such cases and ascribed some convictions to jealousy, petty rivalries, and ineffective legal defenses. Pardons and commutation of sentences were quite common, particularly following the successful conclusion of the war. Reviews undertaken by the office of the army judge advocate general often found the records of wartime courts-martial insufficient or defective and added to those granted reprieves and clemency. Dr. Holder learned of the unjust imprisonment of a number of the inmates and brought their cases to the attention of the authorities, which led in some instances to their release.[23]

As the number of prisoners increased in 1863, record keeping suffered. While earlier reports listed all detainees by name and unit, detailed records were not maintained as increasing numbers arrived. When 105 convicts arrived in April, the clerk noted only that the post had "one hundred & fifteen prisoners undergoing sentence of Ct. Martial of this Post received Aug. 7, '62, Feb. 17, '63, and April 9th '63 respectively." By June the records list 137 prisoners, of which "28 arrived June 28, 1863." By November returns ceased mentioning prisoners by name at all. Two parenthetical entries account for numbers with no detail. The entry "31 prisoners sent to rejoin Regt, died, & escaped during the month" is followed by "130 Prisoners (Enlisted men, citizens, & negroes) received Nov. 3rd & Nov. 22nd respectively."[24] Who the "citizens & negroes" were and what charges had been brought against them remain unknown. Only military tribunals had the option of sending those found guilty to the Tortugas.

Emily Holder noted that "on the 8th of November, 1863, a steamer came in with one hundred and twenty-five prisoners from the prisons at the North, which were running over with bounty jumpers, deserters, and men who had committed a variety of misdemeanors. We heard that Tortugas was going to be made a military prison for our soldiers and were rather dreading it." As it happened, however, the arrival of larger numbers of prisoners coincided with an inability on the part of the engineers to recruit construction laborers from the North. For that reason the convicts were immediately drafted into the Fort Jefferson workforce and labored alongside the slaves and the few craftsmen who still returned to work through the winter months when the climate was less oppressive. "The morning after [the prisoners'] arrival they were drawn up in a line and the overseer of the works took the name of each man, their occupation and trade, then they were turned over to the department they could work in, and as all trades nearly were represented, things began to look brisk again."[25]

5

War's End and the Arrival
of the Conspirators

1864–1865

The sources of military convicts at the Tortugas were mixed. Most prisoners had been convicted of routine kinds of offenses, but alongside these were several emerging from notorious and high-profile cases brought to courts-martial. One such case involved the mutiny at Fort Jackson, Louisiana. Fort Jackson was an isolated coastal defense fort in the delta of the Mississippi River south of New Orleans, manned by one of the new African-American units, the Fourth U.S. Infantry Regiment, Corps d'Afrique. The troubles were caused by the brutal whipping of two black drummer boys by a white officer, second in command of the unit, Lieutenant Colonel Augustus W. Benedict. The whipping was a particularly violent one, inflicted with a raw-hide cart whip. This measure might have been overlooked by the soldiers, primarily former slaves, but Benedict had resorted to violent and severe punishments on many previous occasions. That a high-ranking officer would insist on executing such sentences personally was also calculated to cost him the respect of his subordinates. Following the public spectacle of the whipping, the soldiers were dismissed and returned to their quarters.[1]

One hour later, about half the regiment armed themselves and emerged from the barracks enraged by the punishments. Firing into the air, the mob descended on the guardhouse, freeing the prisoners, and rushed the levee, believing that Colonel Benedict had gone aboard the U.S.S. *Suffolk*. "One man proposed to 'kill all the damned Yankees.'" The disturbance continued for several hours, until the soldiers' white officers calmed the situation and promised that justice would be done. "Soon after, tattoo was beaten, and the men retired to their quarters." In the commission's later analysis, it was concluded that "the conduct of the men was more owing to an ignorance of their rights and the proper means of redress than to any preconcerted plan of revolt."[2]

A court-martial was convened to consider the guilt or innocence of the ringleaders of the riot. The majority of the soldiers were charged with mutiny or insubordinate conduct detrimental to good order and discipline. Five soldiers were found innocent either due to the evidence or due to "conflicting and unsatisfactory" evidence. Six soldiers of the Fourth U.S. Infantry were found guilty and sentenced to terms of from one to twenty years at hard labor to be "carried into execution at Fort Jefferson, Fla.": Musician Edward B. Smith of Company K, one year at hard labor; Corporal Lewis Cady, Company K, two years; Private Charles Taylor, Company K, ten years; Private Abram Singleton, Company F, ten years; Private Willis Curtis, Company D, ten years; and Private Julius Boudro, Company D, twenty years. Two soldiers, Private Frank Williams of Company I and Private Abraham Victoria of Company D, were sentenced to "be shot to death with musketry, at such time and place as the commanding general may direct." Their death sentences were suspended by the convening authorities, and close confinement at the Tortugas was substituted. The final decision of the court-martial was rendered at New Orleans on December 30, 1863. The department provost marshal general ordered that the eight prisoners be transported to Fort Jefferson, where they arrived in March 1864. Lieutenant Colonel Augustus Benedict was convicted of "inflicting cruel and unusual punishment, to the prejudice of good order and military discipline," and was stripped of his commission and expelled from the service of the United States.[3]

Emily Holder recalled that "the new year of 1864 was ushered in with cold winds and rain, so that a fire on the hearth gave us both comfort and company, and during the night more rain fell than in any one day during the year, accompanied by severe thunder and lightning."[4] The next day a steamer arrived with returning veteran troops of the 47th Pennsylvania regiment, who had been authorized leave at their homes. They were visibly healthier and had clearly benefited from their sojourn in a more temperate climate.

On Tuesday, March 1, 1864, the second battalion of the 47th Pennsylvania, consisting of companies E, F, G, and H, was relieved at Fort Jefferson by the 110th New York Volunteer Infantry, which "disembarked from the steamer *Demolay* and came ashore and stacked their arms to await their new quarters to be vacated by the soldiers of the 47th, who boarded the same ship that had brought the 110th to the Tortugas."[5] The ship sailed at noon the next day, ending the 47th Regiment's fourteen months of duty at Garden Key. The first battalion of the 47th serving at Key West was relieved by an African-American unit, the Second Regiment U.S. Colored Troops. The Pennsylvanians were bound for Louisiana, where they were assigned to General Nathaniel Banks's forces on the eve of his unsuccessful Red River Campaign. Colonel Charles Hamilton assumed command of Fort Jefferson the same day. With the arrival of the 110th, the post was manned by a full regiment for the second time, probably due to the increased number of prisoners rather than to any threat of attack on the installation. The New York regiment numbered about 674 soldiers present for duty.[6]

A second detachment of the 110th New York remained behind in New Orleans performing military police, or provost guard, duties. At 5:00 a.m. on March 27 they reported to the parish prison where they took custody of sixty-eight military convicts sentenced to the Tortugas. Among the prisoners at New Orleans were those convicted as a result of the mutiny at Fort Jackson. Sergeant Harrison Herrick recalled that they embarked later that day aboard the steamship *Erickson*, which sailed as far as the mouth of the Mississippi, where it lay at anchor until the next morning waiting on a pilot. Once the ship cleared the delta into deeper waters the weather became windy and a light rain began to fall. They came within sight of Garden Key at 10:00 a.m. on March 30 and anchored about a mile offshore. Captain Doyle and Major Devendorf met the ship and went aboard to arrange for the transfer of the prisoners. By late that afternoon the soldiers and prisoners had been shuttled to the fort in small boats. It was reported that "the garrison was reinforced Mar. 31st, 1864 by the arrival of 33 enlisted men and 4 commissioned officers."[7]

On April 14 the regimental surgeon, Dr. Mitchell, took the precaution of vaccinating the unit against smallpox, knowing the post's unhealthy reputation during the hot summer months; he was probably also responding to the unhealthy condition of many of the prisoners. Sergeant Herrick and two other soldiers, Peter Bartoe and Harvey Kinney, borrowed one of the boats and went fishing on April 24. Herrick reported he had little luck fishing but "got allmighty sick" during the course of the day. The men practiced drills on the heavy artillery guns the next afternoon, the sergeant noting, "I did not feel very well over my fishing voyage." Little changed at Fort Jefferson during the month, although Company K was detached to Key West to serve as the provost guard for the town.[8] May and June were the months that witnessed the return of thousands of sea birds to mate and nest on the nearby keys. Like others stationed on Garden Key, the soldiers of the 110th New York would have supplemented their diet with sea bird eggs.

May 5, 1864, marked the greatest increase in the convict population with the arrival of 280 federal military prisoners from the eastern theater of the war, formerly held at Fort Delaware. Their removal from that installation was made necessary by increasing numbers of Confederate prisoners of war there. The new contingent arrived at Fort Jefferson aboard the U.S.S. *Thames* accompanied by a double guard. The next day, as the prisoners were brought ashore, Sergeant Herrick recorded that there were no formations or drills due to the increased demand for guards. A rumor "was noised about the fort that the prisoners were agoing to rase," which also increased the level of vigilance. By the end of the month 344 convicts had been received, seven had been released, two had died, and three had escaped. The total number of prisoners had increased to 689 by the end of May. After the *Thames* was unloaded a schooner arrived that landed beef cattle on one of the nearby keys. Their ocean voyage and dry fodder at the storage pens meant the average butchered carcass seldom weighed more than three hundred pounds.[9]

Another source of prisoners was added that spring. On May 9, 1864, Secretary of the Navy Gideon Welles directed Rear Admiral D. G. Farragut, commanding the blockade of the Confederacy from New Orleans, that citizens captured in the course of the blockade should be sent "to a Northern port for safer custody unless there is a suitable place for keeping them within the limits of your command." A second memo from Welles ten days later related that the secretary of war "knew of no other place except the Tortugas where there were ample accommodations for the blockade runners." It was not long until these new prisoners began arriving. Admiral Farragut sent Mobile pilot James Campbell to Fort Jefferson in September, describing him as "a notorious blockade runner [who has] been constantly employed running between [Mobile Bay] and Havana."[10]

By June the population was nearly evenly divided: 653 soldiers and 753 convicts. This almost assured increased tension and attempted escapes. Three prisoners were listed as "deserted" that month, probably having successfully stowed away on one of the civilian freighters delivering construction materials. Herrick noted that three more nearly escaped on June 1 in one of the small boats anchored outside the main gate, due to the negligence of the sergeant of the guard, Daniel B. Hunt. Captain James Doyle took a few men aboard a small sailing vessel, the *Rarity*, and after a prolonged pursuit, returned with his captives and the stolen boat. The regiment was being tasked with more duties in the district as time went on, and Colonel Hamilton was in command of both the Tortugas and Key West garrisons. He left Captain Doyle in charge in June, and Major H. C. Devendorf in August and September.[11]

Figure 14. Enclosed casemates used as quarters on southeast curtain 3 in 1864. The guardrooms and sallyport are under the shed roof. Courtesy National Archives, 77F74-79D.

Rising temperatures and unusually severe infestations of bedbugs and mosquitoes drove one prisoner to pen a poetic appeal for relief to the commander of the Department of the Gulf, Major General Nathaniel Banks. Private Thomas Moran of the 11th Indiana Volunteers had been convicted in February 1864 of authoring and circulating a petition demanding the resignation of his company commander, Captain Thomas C. Pursel. The evidence against Moran was later found to be questionable, and probably tainted by the perjury of another soldier. Nevertheless, he was sentenced to one year's hard labor and transported to the Dry Tortugas in late March or early April 1864. On June 5, 1864, Moran composed a desperate plea to General Banks, reading in part:

My voice from Tortugas
I ask you to hear
And to my petition
Deafen not your ear
I ask once again
With my comrades to fight

For the flag and our country
The Union, the Right.

I am no deserter
To be punished so severe
When the call was for duty
I always was there
I never yet flinched
When the foeman was near
My voice from Tortugas
I ask you to hear.

To labor all day
Without comfort of ease
At night go to bed
To be eat by the fleas
Not one ray of hope
The discomfort to cheer
My voice from Tortugas
I ask you to hear.

One year on this island
I must pass away
And beside that must forfeit
One whole year's pay
I write you these lines
From this prison on sea
A pardon I ask
General from thee.

Private Moran's lament and some favorable comments from his unit were sufficient to secure his pardon. The Department of the Gulf published orders on July 14, 1864, for his immediate release and transportation to his unit.[12]

September in the Tortugas was oppressively hot. Sergeant Herrick noted that on the sixth the temperature reached 110 degrees, "the hottest day we had in all summer." The day before, a few of the cattle had been driven into the surf and swam to Garden Key to be butchered. Herrick treated his soldiers to a gallon of whiskey that evening. That small quantity divided between twelve or fifteen men probably does not account for "Stebins the butcher [who] got pretty drunk & Came in our room & raised hell." At the end of the month forty soldiers were hospitalized and twelve prisoners had died of scurvy or tropical fevers.

November 1864 witnessed the peak of the incarcerated population on Garden Key as their numbers swelled to 882. With Company K detached to Key West, the 110th New York had fewer than 583 soldiers available to guard the prisoners. Not surprisingly, five convicts escaped in November and three more in December.[13] November was also the occasion of a great deal of excitement when three misguided sailors from the barque *New York* jumped ship at Garden Key on November 10. One was located almost immediately, but the search for the other two continued for three days. The sailors were able to blend in with the sympathetic convict population and escape detection. Colonel Hamilton was determined to return them to their ship, and on Sunday, November 13, ordered the entire population of prisoners shuttled to Long Key, a nearby low expanse of coral sand, brush, and cactus. Private Henry Whitney recalled that "about 8.o.c. we were all ordered to fall in with our belt & side arms—soon the whole Regt was out to look for the two missing seamen." A thorough inspection of the facility was then conducted. Late in the day Privates J. Van Linder and John Dyer discovered the wayward mariners climbing out of the bakery chimney. The soldiers split a thirty-two-dollar reward for their apprehension. Conditions on the *New York* must have been particularly barbaric to drive crewmembers to prefer escape to an isolated prison over continued service aboard.[14] Private Whitney commented the next day that two prisoners who worked in the bakery "are wearing jewelry [leg irons] to pay for their share in the afare & will wheel brick for a change." A series of northers brought much cooler weather. On November 19 the steamer *Merrimac* arrived with 130 prisoners and the news of President Lincoln's reelection.[15]

Rumors of an African-American regiment relieving the 110th New York proved to be untrue, although the 99th U.S. Colored Troops did stop at Garden Key briefly on their way to Fort Barrancas, Florida. The regiment arrived on January 28, 1865, and departed on February 8. Mrs. Holder commented favorably: "The officers were fine looking men and the privates stalwart healthy negroes, more like real African than any colored people I had ever seen before; they came from Mississippi and Louisiana. They were constantly frolicking and playing games and tricks upon each other, always apparently in the best of humor and evidently very proud of being soldiers." The 99th was a newly formed unit, however, and did have its discipline problems. One soldier was insubordinate and resisted arrest, leading to his being shot and wounded by guard Corporal Lewis A. Erskine.[16]

One incident in March 1865 would lead one to question Dr. Holder's credentials as either a man of science or a naturalist. A number of his "experiments" resembled the pranks of a fraternity house more than the sober observations of a scientist. The doctor, along with a crew of prisoners that included "Fat Charley" Rodgers, had captured a large "man eating" shark in the nearby shallows and were determined to convert the filthy moat into an aquarium. A great deal of effort was expended hauling the shark over the counterscarp and into the enclosed waters. Holder recalled: "The shark was regarded as equal to several sentinels; for the prisoners, who were quartered in the casemates above the moat, would hardly dare to swim across." The soldiers nicknamed the shark "Provost Marshal" and noted the effect it had on the convicts. The shark silently patrolled the moat from end to end with one beady eye on the wall or breakwater. "He was kept without food for a while in view of having a grand show at his first meal. Sundry cats were to be fed out to him."[17]

The time for the spectacle of shark feeding came in the twilight following retreat on Sunday, March 19, 1865. The starving "man eater" was slowly patrolling the moat as a large crowd of soldiers and convicts assembled on the ramparts or peered through the embrasures. Dr. Holder and engineer Edward Frost stood on the breakwater to ensure an unobstructed view of the carnage. Fat Charley stood above on the ramparts, with a very large cat and a number of ox feet supplied by the butcher. On Dr. Holder's signal, the cat was launched off the rampart and fell fifty feet into the moat directly in front of the oncoming shark. Contrary to expectations, the shark, unaccustomed to that method of food delivery, turned tail and swam away at a smart pace. Hisses and cries of "humbug," and "we want our money back," came from the crowd. The cat, unharmed, swam nearly the length of the moat and was finally rescued by some prisoners who let down a rope tied to an old shirt. Clawing its way onto the shirt, the cat was hauled inside to safety amid cheers from the convicts. Mrs. Devendorf, the commandant's wife and evidently a woman fond of cats, was quite put out by the entire sorry spectacle and made her feelings known.[18]

The conclusion of the war was an occasion for celebration at Fort Jefferson. Sergeant Herrick noted in his diary: "April Thursday 20th [1865] The steamer *Corinthian* came in from Key West & brought news that Gen. Lee & his hold army was captured. She also had on board a troop of minstrels that performed at 12 m [noon] in the new commissary storehouse at 2 p.m. there was a brass band came ashore & played a national air, we commenced to fire a salute of 200 guns in honor of the victory."[19] Lee's surrender to

Figure 15. View to the north with the officer quarters to the left and enlisted men's barracks to the right. This is one of four photos taken by engineer Edward Frost and submitted with the 1864 annual construction report. Courtesy National Archives, 77F74-79C.

General Grant was quickly followed by the defeat of General Joseph Johnston in North Carolina and the surrender of the Trans-Mississippi Confederacy by General Edmund Kirby Smith at Galveston, Texas, on June 2, 1865.

Emily Holder recalled receiving the news of Lincoln's assassination. "But while in the midst of our rejoicing, never dreaming of anything but continued cheering news, the *Ella Morse* came in with the flag at half-mast and the terrible announcement of the tragedy at Washington. . . . Half-hour guns . . . pronounced it a day of mourning, and a weight hung over us for days; we could not, if we would throw it off. Every joy and victory seemed dwarfed by this horrible act, and we could talk or think of little else."[20] A few of the convicts tried to celebrate Lincoln's passing, but the sentry fired a round over their heads and they were subsequently tied up outside the guardhouse. Private Whitney recorded that one of the prisoners celebrating Lincoln's murder "was strung up so long that he died soon arfter being cut down. I honestly confess that I have very little sympathy for him or any man who is punished for such expressions."[21] To say that Abraham Lincoln became a martyr to the Union cause would be very much an understatement. The nation entered a protracted period of mourning.

Prior to the arrival of the conspirators convicted by military commissions for their alleged involvement in the assassination of President Abraham Lincoln, there had been no suggestion of cruelty, torture, or abuse of prisoners in the Dry Tortugas. This statement requires an examination of nineteenth-century standards and accepted methods for enforcing military discipline as well as of punishments for violations of law and regulations. Punishments for the latter in the U.S. Army dated back to the formative years of the Revolutionary War and remained virtually unchanged at the time of the Civil War. During that early period arrest or confinement was not considered a punishment but only a necessary condition to ensure that the accused would be present for trial.

Punishment by that standard was understood to take two broad forms, corporal or capital. Minor infractions resulted in "extra duty," merely additional duty hours beyond those of the routine for the soldier's unit. Other common punishments at Fort Jefferson, and typical of practices at the time, included being tied to a scaffold by the thumbs, known to the soldiers as being placed in *durance vile*, or an extreme trial of endurance. Private Henry Whitney of the 110th New York mentions an instance in March 1864 of this being inflicted on a member of his company who failed to perform guard duty correctly.[22] Another common punishment was to "carry the ball." Soldiers would be required to carry a solid cannonball weighing from twenty-four to over one hundred pounds for two hours at a time around a path on the parade field. Hauling sand from one location to another and relocating piles of heavy construction timbers were also penalties related to the ongoing construction. It is important to realize that all of these methods of corporal punishment were entirely public and visible to soldiers, civilian workers, and families; they were an accepted fixture of military life.

By modern standards, a high degree of physical brutality was also acceptable during military training. Doctrine at that time gave officers and noncommissioned officers responsible for training recruits only one methodology to combine tactical training and physical training and to instill discipline. That single method was close-order drill. It was common to drill new soldiers for between two and four hours at a time. The physical demands of marching, facing movements, and "quick time"—marching at a jogging pace with a heavy musket—were often beyond the physical capabilities of new recruits. It was not unusual for sergeants to inspire the reluctant with

Figure 16. View to the west across the parade with foundations of the barracks in the foreground. Photo by Paulien Reid.

cuffs, kicks, or blows with the butt of a rifle. Ideally such training produced proficient soldiers with the endurance to withstand nineteenth-century warfare. Predictably it also produced men who were discharged for inability or medical disability. Given the large number of illiterates, immigrants, and soldiers with chronic undiagnosed disease, sergeants were challenged equally by training volunteers or conscripts.

None of this is intended to justify an outmoded, brutal tradition of military law or discipline. It is a warning to avoid anachronism in judging history by a modern set of standards that did not exist at the time. During the years following the war a number of serious accusations were made against officers and soldiers responsible for the prisoners at the Dry Tortugas. The ethical standards of many of the reporters and newspapers that sensationalized these allegations are also open to question. Other factors that should be considered include the claims of innocence of all four of the so-called conspirators, their conviction by a military tribunal under conditions later ruled unconstitutional by the U.S. Supreme Court, and the total unfamiliarity of the four with military life. In sum, these facts led to fears of conspiracy, persecution, and being singled out for harsh treatment.

An incident in July 1865 again raised the tensions between the engineers and the garrison commander. An engineer overseer evidently involved in an unauthorized private enterprise used convict labor to move a herd of his swine from Long Key to Bird Key, to profit from better forage. The island was also the site of numerous graves of Union soldiers who had died at the fort. This was seen as an outrage by commander Major Henry Devendorf, since the graves were necessarily shallow, and the hogs would inevitably root up the recently departed. Civil engineer Edward Frost agreed that the pigs would be returned to their range on Long Key but complained that Devendorf had authorized cattle to be penned on the parade of Fort Jefferson where the animals had damaged valuable shade trees. Frost insisted that the cattle pens should also be relocated to Long Key. Both Major Devendorf and his successors ignored Frost's request; when a hurricane struck three months later, the walls of the pens were blown over, releasing the cattle to wander on the parade.[23]

Under a pall of federal secrecy, the four men convicted for complicity in the assassination of the president were removed from prisons near the Capitol and placed in irons below decks of the gunboat U.S.S. *Florida*. Dr. Samuel A. Mudd, Michael O'Laughlin, Samuel Bland Arnold, and Edman Spangler arrived at the pier at Fort Jefferson on July 24, 1865. The killing of Abraham Lincoln had produced near hysteria in the newspapers of the day, fostering belief in a broad conspiracy with the perpetrators ranging from the Confederate government at Richmond to the Roman Catholic Church. Barely three months passed between the shooting by John Wilkes Booth and the arrival of the surviving accused at Fort Jefferson. They were truly the most notorious criminals in America. Private Henry B. Whitney of the 110th New York described the scene: "About noon a large steamer came in sight & signaled for a pilot shurly we thought our relief had come but soon she showed unmistakable signs of being a gunboat & so it proved for we soon found it was the U.S. Gunboat *Florida* with the *conspiters* ... considerable stir when the prisoners looked on the little rock . . . I wonder if they will ever get off this key[.] Time will tell."[24] Extensive publicity ensured that the unfortunate group would have been recognized wherever they had gone. Whitney commented, "They answer the descriptions we have had of them well at least so that I picked them out as they came up."[25]

Samuel Arnold described their arrival. "We were now left under the charge of Col. Charles Hamilton, One Hundred Tenth New York Volunteers, who was at that period commandant of the post. He gave us instructions relative to the rules in force, stating the consequences which would

Figure 17. Note the complex multiple arches in second tier casemates. Many were designed by Captain Daniel P. Woodbury, who published a monograph on arch construction in 1858; photo circa 1900. Courtesy National Archives, 200M90-1-10.

attend any breach in discipline, finally impressing upon our minds that there was a dark and gloomy dungeon within the fort, to which offenders against the rules were consigned, over whose entrances was inscribed the classic words: 'Whoso entereth here leaveth all hope behind.'"[26]

Emily Holder later described Dr. Mudd as restless and brooding. She recalled: "He asked my husband to send a long letter, which he gave him to read, to the New York 'Herald'—a very sensational and untrue report of the treatment of the prisoners. He had imagined all sorts of indignities and persecutions, when, in fact, they were treated to the same conditions and surroundings as the soldiers." There is no evidence the letter was ever published. To give Mudd some useful activity, Dr. Holder employed him as an aide in the hospital. Arnold related that Mudd had relocated from his earlier quarters to a cot in the ward. Holder evidently placed considerable trust in him, but on one occasion this had unfortunate results. The enlisted hospital steward, W. W. Wythe, asked Mudd to dispense medication to two patients while he went to the mess hall for dinner. Dr. Mudd mistakenly gave the men a very strong and irritating laxative rather than the treatment for diarrhea that had been ordered.[27]

Figure 18. View to the west across the parade toward bastion F and west curtain 5 in 1864. Engineer lumber and paint sheds are in the foreground. Courtesy National Archives, 77F74-79B.

By the time the steward returned the two men were in extreme discomfort, and Dr. Holder was called. He discovered the error and administered an antidote that relieved the men's suffering. The officers learned of the incident and were convinced that it had been intentional, but Holder finally persuaded them that this could not have been the case, since Mudd had absolutely nothing to gain from it. Nevertheless, such carelessness could not be allowed in a hospital, and Dr. Mudd was removed and put to other duties.

In a letter to his brother-in-law he omitted the actual reason for his dismissal from the clinic, stating: "I don't regret the loss of my position. Take away the honor attached, the labor was more confining than any other place or avocation on the island. At the same time it relieved me of the disagreeable necessity of witnessing men starve for the nutriment essential for a sick man, when it could be had with no trouble and but a little expense." Mudd contended that the deaths of four prisoners while he was employed in the hospital were somehow symptomatic of neglect. "Not a single soldier or citizen laborer has died or suffered with any serious sickness; thereby showing something wrong, something unfair, and a distinction made between the two classes of individuals."[28]

Emily Holder's observations of the treatment of the state prisoners were generally positive. Regarding Samuel Arnold she wrote:

> The youngest of the state prisoners so won the sympathies of the colonel's wife [Mrs. Hamilton], by his illness and thorough submission, that she prevailed upon the colonel to put him at some duty more congenial. He was installed as a clerk in the office, and without doubt the young fellow had many a lunch from a home table the colonel knew nothing about, or was willing to trust the generous heart of his wife in her unmilitary insubordination. I heard her remark one day: 'I could not see that boy dying from homesickness and the want of a little care, when by management, which I alone am responsible for, it can be averted,' and his appearance before many weeks bore evidence of kindly interest.[29]

Arnold confirmed this in his *Memoirs*, saying, "Soon leg irons were introduced, and each [state prisoner] ironed, with the exception of myself, they remaining off me, because I was engaged in writing for some of the officers at post headquarters."[30]

General George Armstrong Custer provided the Dry Tortugas with another prisoner under life sentence who arrived on September 13, 1865. Custer had been assigned to Reconstruction duty in Texas and was assembling a cavalry division for that purpose near Alexandria, Louisiana, in June 1865. One of the units assigned to the new division was the 2nd Wisconsin Volunteer Cavalry. With the war at an end, the volunteers had no stomach for continued service. Many soldiers deserted, refused duty, or became seriously insubordinate. One soldier with an excellent war record and reputation, Sergeant Leonard Lee Lancaster of Company L, began circulating a petition to encourage their unpopular regimental commander to resign and go home. While volunteer units were allowed to elect their officers, calling on one to resign was mutiny. Custer, unable to establish order within the volunteer regiments, decided to make an example of a captured deserter and Sergeant Lancaster. A court-martial was convened; both men were found guilty and sentenced to death.

On the day of the execution the division was formed in a three-sided square with the offenders and the firing squad in the center. The two soldiers were hooded and seated on their coffins. General Custer sat mounted as the orders "Ready" and "Aim" were given to the firing squad. Before the order to "Fire" was issued, he directed that Lancaster should be led away.

The deserter was executed, and Sergeant Lancaster's sentence was commuted to life at hard labor in the Dry Tortugas. These extreme punishments did nothing to change attitudes in the volunteer regiments. They continued to be insubordinate and uncooperative until they were later mustered out in Texas.[31]

On August 1, 1865, the long-awaited relief arrived for the 110th New York Volunteers. Captain William R. Prentice of the 161st New York relieved Colonel Alexander and took command. The commander of the 161st, Lieutenant Colonel William B. Kinsey, was absent on detached service at Fort Barrancas, Florida, and Major Willis E. Craig had been detailed as commander of the garrison at Key West. Private Henry Whitney was not impressed by the new unit. He commented, "The other Regt made rather an awkward performance mounting guard for *old soldiers*." Whatever its deficiencies, the soldiers of the 110th were elated to see the new unit. They departed Fort Jefferson on August 16 aboard the steamer *Tonawanda* out of New Orleans bound for New York and home.[32]

The changes among the garrison probably resulted in significant breaches of security due to the inexperience of the new arrivals. One civilian prisoner named John W. Adare, convicted of robbery and described as desperate and reckless, planned an escape that contained elements of each. Accompanied by a black companion, Adare slipped away one night and recovered some hidden planks. Floating on the planks, the two managed to paddle nearly three miles through waters infested with sharks attracted to the hides and offal dumped offshore when animals were butchered. Guided by the lighthouse, they reached Loggerhead Key, where they stole the keeper's boat and began the ninety-mile journey to Havana. After arriving safely, Adare implemented a second plan to secure funds for his passage to Europe. He advertised his traveling companion for sale, noting that in addition to a bargain price, the slave had added value due to his experience as a skilled sailor.

The black man, discovering Adare's generous offer, informed the Spanish authorities of the true circumstances. Although there was no treaty of extradition between the two nations, the Spaniards evidently believed that the United States should continue to bear the expense of the pair's imprisonment. The fugitives were placed in chains on a ship bound for Key West, where the Cubans released them to the American military authorities. After being returned to Fort Jefferson, Adare was fitted with an ankle chain and ball weighing some thirty pounds. In spite of that, eighteen months later Adare escaped a second time to Loggerhead Key using an additional plank to support the weight of the ball and chain. He found, however, that the lighthouse keeper's boat was locked securely in an outbuilding. He was found hidden in the dense brush and prickly pear cactus the next day by the corporal's guard and was again returned to Garden Key.[33]

Emily Holder later recalled a chance meeting with Edman Spangler. He "was a carpenter, and was sent one day with some other workmen to do a little work at our house. I could not resist speaking to him. He said, with perfect good nature: 'They made a mistake sending me down here. I had nothing to do with Booth or the assassination of President Lincoln; but I suppose I have done enough in my life to deserve this, so I make the best of it.'" Of the four conspirators confined at Garden Key, Spangler was probably the least culpable. The military commission had convicted him of assisting in Booth's escape despite the fact that Spangler was unaware at the time that President Lincoln had been shot.[34]

Dr. Samuel A. Mudd wrote early in September 1865 that "a transport has just arrived and will take off at least a hundred prisoners, thereby thinning our ranks considerably."[35] Prisoners released that month numbered 132. Mudd's concern for his personal welfare was heightened with the arrival of the 82nd U.S. Colored Troops on September 12, 1865. The unit was commanded by Major George E. Wentworth. The 161st New York Volunteer Infantry was mustered out and eventually departed for home aboard the steam transport *Thomas A. Scott*. On September 25 Dr. Mudd attempted to stow away on the same vessel as the volunteers but was quickly discovered. Mudd wrote that six other prisoners made good their escape aboard the ship, but the official record mentions the escape of only two convicts. Later investigations suggest that the two had been provided with uniforms and were hidden by some soldiers of the departing regiment; the prisoners were never apprehended.

Early in October 1865 Henry Kelly, a sailor who assisted Dr. Mudd in his escape attempt, was incarcerated but escaped after dislodging the rusted bars from the window of his cell. In his report of the incident ordered by Department Headquarters Brigadier General Newton stated: "Kelly the accomplice of Mudd in his attempted escape tore away the iron bars from the window, and escaped in a boat of the Engineer Department hauled out [of the water] for repairs." Newton left instructions that all such boats should be guarded in the future.[36] The prisoner population had declined by the end of October to 393.

Another state prisoner, Colonel George St. Leger Grenfell, arrived on October 8, 1865. He had been convicted by a military tribunal of involvement in the "Chicago Conspiracy" to free Confederate prisoners of war from Camp Douglas. Grenfell was a British soldier of fortune who had served with the Confederacy as adjutant to General John Hunt Morgan in Kentucky and Tennessee. Shortly after Grenfell's arrival, Brigadier General John Newton, commander of the District of Middle Florida, and Brigadier General J. W. Forsythe inspected Fort Jefferson and Wentworth's troops on October 20 and 21, leaving behind new instructions for an increased level of security for the state prisoners.[37]

On Sunday, October 22, increasing north winds brought soaking rain throughout the day. That evening about 9:00 p.m. engineer clerk John Barker crossed the parade, finding uprooted trees and loose cattle, their pens having been blown down. The hurricane increased in intensity during the night. Shortly after midnight the front wall of the three-story brick officer quarters under construction collapsed into the interior of the building. Soldiers, officers, and their families began leaving their quarters and taking shelter in the casemates as roofing was blown away and torrents of rain poured in. The storm was at its worst just before dawn on Monday morning.[38]

At about 5:00 a.m. the rear wall of the unfinished officer quarters collapsed outward onto a small kitchen building, killing Quartermaster John W. Sterling and seriously injuring Captain R. A. Stearns, Company D, who occupied those temporary quarters. Major Wentworth reported: "At the time the wall fell it was blowing a fearful Hurricane; the oldest residents of the Key say that they had not as severe a gale since 1846." The remaining brick wall was unstable, threatening to fall and worsen the damage. Two prisoners volunteered to climb it and attach a large rope so that it could be pulled down. Wentworth stated that they did this "at the risk of their lives, and were conspicuous all day for the manner in which they worked." As a result of their heroism during the storm, Major Wentworth recommended pardons for prisoner Charles C. "Fat Charley" Rogers of Company E, 3rd Vermont Volunteer Infantry, and William H. Griffen, 13th Veteran Reserve Corps. Headquarters quickly approved the requests.[39]

Besides destruction of the unfinished officer quarters considerable structural damage was done to the fort. The existing officer quarters lost much slate roofing and "almost every room in the building was thoroughly saturated with water." The high winds carried the potentially lethal heavy slate fragments seventy-five yards from the structure. Many of the large tropical trees on the parade were uprooted and blown around like straws. Twenty of the wooden walls enclosing the second tier of casemates occupied by the enlisted soldiers were blown out, allowing the quarters to be flooded by wind-driven rain. On top of the ramparts the roofs blew off the heavy guns, one landing in the middle of the parade ground 411 yards away. Long Key had been reduced in size by nearly half, and the hogs had been swept away by the surf. It took the engineers nearly a year to recover from the effects of the hurricane.

The tempest also struck three vessels bringing workers and materials to Fort Taylor and Garden Key. The steamer *Governor Marvin*, out of New York, was carrying 150 workmen and engineer Edward Frost to Fort Taylor. The ship was battered by huge waves in the open Atlantic off Cape Canaveral, Florida, killing two workers. The schooner *Nelly Barrett*, heavily loaded with steel beams and construction materials, foundered and was lost at sea. A bark, the *Aegean*, also sailing from New York, weathered the storm and safely delivered two hundred workmen to Fort Jefferson. The faithful engineer schooner *Tortugas* was caught by the killer storm at the quartermaster wharf at Key West. The storm surge and waves drove the ship against the pilings, crushed the bulkheads, and sank it. Later, after receiving reports from John Barker at Fort Jefferson and Edward Frost at Fort Taylor, Captain McFarland concluded that damage from the storm amounted to $25,000. Nearly one year later in September 1866, he reported that the officer quarters that had collapsed had been rebuilt and the roof beams were in place.[40]

At least partially as a result of Dr. Mudd's escape attempt, Brigadier General John Newton, commander of the District of Middle Florida, published a special order October 20, 1865, setting out "rules and regulations for the safe custody of prisoners," in part forbidding any prisoner to possess more than three dollars in cash at any time. Inmates who received larger sums from friends or relatives were required to place it on deposit with the commanding officer. Due to the limited variety and poor quality of the available rations, prisoners with the means to do so lived largely off goods purchased from the sutler. This was generally not an option for the majority of the convicts and private soldiers. General Newton's orders also gave the commander "full control over the mails, sent by or to be delivered to prisoners." Probably the most galling to Dr. Mudd and the other conspirators was paragraph four, which stated: "Prisoners of State will not be allowed outside of the Fort. When out of the dungeon always to be under Guard, with leg irons. A Sentinel will always be placed over the dungeon."[41]

Samuel Arnold's later lengthy account of these regulations is a study in paranoia. He was convinced that every action that was prejudicial to the "state prisoners" had its origin with Secretary of War Edwin Stanton and Judge Advocate General Joseph Holt. His explanation of the reasoning that led to these conclusions was clear but revealed ignorance of the workings of army administration. A recurring problem with the volunteer regiments serving at Fort Jefferson involved their failure to segregate garrison or installation records from those of their units. There is little doubt that when they departed, both the 110th New York and the 161st New York volunteers removed the files related to rules governing the prisoners as well as removing their own files. Lieutenant Colonel Lewis Tinelli of the 90th New York had complained of the same practice when he assumed command in June of 1862. It was for these reasons that Major George E. Wentworth of the 82nd U.S. Colored Troops had no established rules for treatment of prisoners when he assumed command on September 12, 1865.

Dr. Samuel Mudd's escape attempt less than two weeks later revealed fatal flaws in the fort's security arrangements. Mudd had changed from his coarse prison flannel clothing and dressed in a suit and linen shirt. Probably aided by soldiers of the 161st New York Volunteers, he passed through the gate onto the pier where the New Yorkers were preparing to board their transport to return to their homes. With the assistance of a member of the ship's crew, Henry Kelly, whom the doctor had probably bribed with cash, Mudd was concealed below decks under some loose planking in the hold. It was at that point that routine security procedures became effective. Before any ship sailed, a muster formation for the prisoners was held, and this time several convicts were discovered to be absent; all attention was focused on Mudd, given his prominent status. A thorough search of the *Thomas A. Scott* was conducted, leading to the discovery of the doctor when Lieutenant Arthur Tappan probed the planks of the hold with his saber. An imaginative engraving in the October 21, 1865, edition of *Harper's Weekly*, allegedly inspired by a drawing made by one of the passengers aboard the ship, shows the lieutenant with a lantern as he discovers Mudd's feet protruding from the barrel of a large cannon. It is probably unnecessary to say that a transport like the *Scott* did not have any armaments large enough to accommodate a human body. Dr. Mudd was temporarily placed in the guardhouse wearing leg restraints to prevent another such attempt. The inevitable firestorm of high-level criticism of the new commandant and his management of the convicts was swift and intense as news of the escape reached the nation's capital.

Figure 19. View across parade circa 1900 toward the enlisted men's barracks and 1876 lighthouse, with kitchen buildings in the foreground. Courtesy National Archives, 200M90-1-5.

The War Department, pressured no doubt by radical Republican members of Congress, ordered a full investigation by Major General Philip Sheridan, commanding the Department of the Gulf. Sheridan tasked Brigadier General John G. Foster, commander of the Department of Florida, with the inquiry. Foster visited the Tortugas on October 14, leaving instructions that the state prisoners should be placed in close confinement when not at work. Foster also ordered his subordinate Brigadier General John Newton of the District of Middle Florida to make an inspection and assist Major Wentworth with security procedures and arrangements.[42]

Newton arrived at Fort Jefferson on October 20 and made a thorough inspection of the 82nd U.S. Colored Troops, the installation, and the prisoners. Major Wentworth explained that he had been left no special orders relating to the state prisoners. That evening General Newton returned to his transport, the steamer *Perry*, anchored in the harbor off the fort. His staff drafted an unnumbered special order to address the specific shortcomings that had led to the attempted escape by Mudd and the successful escapes of his accomplice Henry Kelly and a convict named Smith, whom Mudd described as "one of the most outrageous thieves that ever walked." While the orders were clearly the source of strict confinement and discomfort for the state prisoners, they cannot be interpreted to be any part of a larger "conspiracy" to subject these prisoners to torment, as Samuel Arnold would later contend. Any reasonable person would have recognized that their restraint was a matter of national interest, unlike the situation of the common prison population of military deserters, bounty jumpers, and insubordinates.

The publication of the general orders on the spot also allowed General Newton to report truthfully to General Sheridan on October 21 that every issue raised by Mudd's attempt, as well as by the escape of Kelly and Smith, was covered by standing orders then in effect at Fort Jefferson. Newton was probably assisted by Brigadier General J. W. Forsythe, Sheridan's inspector general, who was conducting his own inspection of the garrison at Garden Key at that time. It is clear though, that although some of the measures can be described as common sense, each item in the new regulations can be traced to a fact that had come to light as a result of the recent escapes and attempted escape.[43]

Colonel Grenfell's later contentions of good behavior and his status as the victim of vindictive officers are called into question by impressions gained by Emily Holder.

> Among the last prisoners were some notable characters. Some of them were said to be hotel burners who had tried that as a weapon of devastation in the North, in Chicago and other places. [Grenfell] was a ferocious looking man, six feet tall, black hair, unkempt, long beard, with black eyes under very heavy eyebrows. He wore a red flannel shirt open low on his chest, showing a strong muscular figure, trousers tucked in his high boots, altogether having the appearance of a bandit; and, besides he was wanting in a certain respect of manner that most of the prisoners observed to the ladies and officers whom they met on the walks.

She commented that "the spirit of defiance stood out like porcupine quills in every look and gesture."

Grenfell's habitual violations of the rules ensured that he spent much of his time in the guardhouse and had to perform menial duties during the day, accompanied by a sergeant. "He was so belligerent that a watch had to be kept over him, fearing his influence over other and weaker men."[44]

Four companies of the Fifth U.S. Artillery arrived on November 10, 1865. Brigadier General Bennett H. Hill assumed command on November 12 in accordance with the War Department's General Order 144 of October 9, 1865. Hill had earlier served at Fort Jefferson with Major Arnold in March 1861 as commander of Battery M, 1st U.S. Artillery. Four companies of the 82nd U.S. Colored Troops departed on November 26, but due to the low personnel strength of the Fifth Artillery, four more companies remained at the post. Second Lieutenant Joseph Keeffe of the Fifth Artillery was appointed provost marshal for the prisoners. Dr. Mudd related in a letter to his brother-in-law on November 11: "Yesterday, the 10th, four companies of heavy artillery arrived to relieve the detested and abominable negro regiment, and I am in hopes our future treatment will be much milder."[45] Mudd's hostility to the black soldiers was entirely without basis in fact. Samuel Arnold later wrote: "We did not think it possible that worse men could be found upon the face of the earth than most of the [white] officers connected with the Eighty-second United States Colored Infantry, but we soon found that we had traded off the witch for the devil. As for the enlisted men, or private soldiers, both white and black, I must say that we were treated by them with the utmost kindness and consideration, which shall ever be remembered with the most grateful feelings."[46] It was typical of southern sensitivities in the immediate aftermath of the war to react in the strongest terms to any suggestion of African-Americans being placed on equal terms with whites or even superior to whites, as was the case with the guards and sergeants of the 82nd U.S. Colored Troops.

As of the end of December 1865 Companies D, I, L, and M of the Fifth U.S. Artillery only had 139 soldiers present for duty. Nearly 260 soldiers of the unit had been discharged at the end of their terms of service following the war's end. This was why the four companies of the 82nd U.S. Colored Troops were retained at the post, as noted, with an additional 331 soldiers. The population of prisoners continued to decline, reaching 273 by the end of the year, but the presence of the state prisoners required that a full battalion of guards remain stationed at Fort Jefferson.[47]

On December 22, 1865, Mrs. Frances Mudd wrote a lengthy letter to President Andrew Johnson complaining of Dr. Mudd's treatment, particularly as regards the poor quality of his food and the orders that his legs should remain shackled at all times. She also complained that he was being placed "at hard labor," a charge that was unsupported even by her husband's own letters. These complaints eventually led in January 1866 to correspondence from the War Department directing that if Dr. Mudd's wife's allegations were correct, the prisoners were to be relieved of their chains at once. That sort of high-level interference in the day-to-day management of the fort and its prison population made life difficult for the commandant and often countermanded commonsense measures ordered locally.[48]

Despite the loud protestations of mistreatment, the four Lincoln conspirators had been allowed to receive packages containing clothing, tobacco,

Figure 20. Granite spiral bastion staircases were swept and sanded daily by Dr. Mudd during much of his tenure at Garden Key. The sand absorbed tobacco juice. Photo by Paulien Reid.

and other items that qualified as luxuries in any prison. Mudd noted in a letter to his wife on December 23 that "we have our Christmas dinner already in prospect, [for example]: canned roast turkey, sausage, oysters, preserves, fresh peaches, tomatoes, etc."[49] As the year ended, the Tortugas also experienced cooler weather with several northers making their way through the Gulf.

The Nation's Most Notorious Prison

1866–1868

Far from the prewar perception of Fort Jefferson as an American Gibraltar or the "key to the Gulf," soldiers stationed there following the great conflict had a difficult time imagining why it existed at all. One who served with the Fifth U.S. Artillery concluded; "The only use, it seems to me, that is or can be made of the fort, is that which it really serves at present—as a prison. But whether it was, in the first place, worth while to erect such a structure, for such a purpose, in such a climate, entailing also the necessity of a battalion of soldiers, equally prisoners with those they guard, I leave to wiser heads to determine."[1] Many years later Samuel Arnold recalled that when the "Lincoln conspirators" were informed their destination was the Dry Tortugas, "of it I had no idea beyond that gathered through the columns of the press, in which it had been depicted as a perfect hell, which fact was duly established by imprisonment on its limited space."[2]

The year 1866 at the Tortugas began with a visit to the prisoners by Bishop Verot of Savannah, Georgia, and Father William O'Hara. Dr. Mudd wrote to tell his wife with evident satisfaction that he had been allowed to go to confession and to attend mass and communion. He commented: "There are many Catholics among the [Irish] citizen laborers, and we have quite a large congregation, nearly all going to communion."[3] In a letter three weeks later, his positive tone was replaced by a long inventory of complaints.

> Imagine one loaded down with heavy chains, locked up in a wet, damp room, twelve hours out of every twenty-four during working days and all day on Sundays and holidays. No exercise allowed except in the limited space of a small room, and with irons on. The atmosphere we breathe is highly impregnated with sulphuric hydrogen gas, which you are aware is highly injurious to health as well as disagreeable. The gas is generated by the numerous sinks [latrines] that empty into that portion of the sea enclosed by the breakwater, and which is immedi-

ately under a small port hole—the only admission for air and light we have from the external port. My legs and ankles are swollen and sore, pains in my shoulders and back are frequent. My hair began falling out some time ago, and to save which I shaved it all over clean, and have continued to do so once every week since. . . . With all this, imagine my gait with a bucket and broom, and a guard, walking around from one corner of the Fort to another, sweeping and sanding down the bastions. This has been our treatment for the last three months, coupled with bad diet, bad water, and every inconvenience.[4]

Engineer surgeon Dr. Joseph Holder and his family had left in December 1865 for an assignment at Fort Monroe, Virginia, but he returned to the Tortugas as an "Acting Assistant Surgeon under contract" in May 1866 with the understanding that he would remain through the summer months.[5] Holder was completing his marine biology research for the Smithsonian Institution, which was later published as a series of articles in *Harper's Weekly*. He was also "acclimated," or immune to yellow fever, and had extensive experience in treating that dreaded disease.

Many of the soldiers and prisoners on Garden Key suffered from chronic conjunctivitis from exposure to the tropical sun reflecting from the white coral sand that formed the island. Samuel Arnold observed that it "had a very injurious effect upon the eyes in many cases, causing men to become totally blind after dark, a disease known there and of frequent occurrence, termed moon-blind." The cure was, of course, avoidance of the cause, an accommodation unavailable to soldiers on duty and prisoners serving a sentence of hard labor. The condition was referred to as "ophthalmia" in medical documents of the period. Repeated or prolonged exposure could cause permanent damage. Dr. Mudd complained in January 1866, "My eyesight is beginning to grow very bad, so much so that I can't read or write by candlelight. During the day, owing to the overpowering light and heat, my eyes are painful and irritated, and I can't view any object many seconds without having to close or shade them from the light."[6]

Despite the cooler weather and healthier conditions Sergeant Patrick Craven of Company L, Fifth Artillery, died of disease on January 23, and five other soldiers were listed at the end of the month as disabled. This may have been the result of a lack of medical attention. Dr. Holder had left for Fort Monroe in December at a time when the Fifth Artillery had no medical officer present. This was resolved by the arrival of Surgeon John A. Bell late in January. The 82nd U.S. Colored Troops remained the largest unit

Figure 21. The cell traditionally believed to have been occupied by Dr. Samuel Mudd. In the foreground are two 24-pounder howitzers; photo May 1898. Courtesy National Archives 200M90-3B-84.

serving on Garden Key with 331 present for duty. As we have seen, complaints to President Andrew Johnson by Frances Mudd that her husband was working in chains led to instructions from the War Department that such restraints were uncalled for and their use should be discontinued. General Hill ordered that state prisoners be unshackled and moved to better quarters. Dr. Mudd related in a letter on January 28 that he was "relieved of the horrible chains."[7]

In February prisoners were being released at a more rapid rate, and fewer were arriving; by the end of the month only 207 remained. Dr. Mudd wrote that month that "our quarters [were] changed to a healthier locality, and our fare much improved, so I have hopes of a prolongation of the thread of life."[8] Using the casemates for living quarters for the soldiers and prisoners was ultimately unhealthy. The heavy masonry walls were filled with sand and coral that retained moisture. They were continuously damp and prone to the accumulation of mold and fungus. The addition of wooden walls to the open side of the casemates facing the parade made problems with humidity even worse. Other aggravations came from "having as companions in our misery every insect known to abound on the island, in the shape of mosquitoes, bedbugs, roaches and scorpions, by which, both night and day, we were tormented."[9] Garden Key was also populated with rats that had initially arrived in construction materials. Large numbers of domestic cats probably kept them in check during the nineteenth century.

Incidents in March suggest that sewage from the defective latrines and drains was contaminating the water stored in some of the underground cisterns. Disease was widespread; thirty-eight soldiers were hospitalized and two died. Private Osborn Paydan, of the 82nd Colored Troops, Company F, died of typhoid fever and Private Albert Bibb of Company E of dysentery. The cause was probably bacterial contamination with cholera, a disease with symptoms quite similar to those of typhoid and dysentery. Dr. Mudd mentioned an epidemic of yellow fever and cholera "prevailing at Key West about sixty miles distant." On April 27 he complained: "We are under guard all the time, and no exercise allowed except in the performance of duty, which is very light. I can perform all I have to do in a couple of hours. . . . My duty is simply to sweep down the bastions once every day."[10] By May seventy soldiers were listed as sick. On May 15 the Fifth U.S. Artillery was reinforced by 224 recruits from Carlisle Barracks, Pennsylvania. That allowed the Department of Florida, now short of troops due to the discharge of volunteers, to reassign Company F of the 82nd to Tallahassee for Reconstruction duties.

Drunkenness and alcohol abuse among the soldiers were documented on a number of occasions since being drunk was a violation of orders and often the occasion for punishments. Allegations against officers are more isolated, although certainly present in the records. Private Henry Whitney made some allegations against one of the quartermaster officers of the 110th New York, saying he was a "sot" and accusing him (presumably only in diary entries) of supporting his drunken habits by diverting part of the men's rations in exchange for liquor.[11] In his history of the 47th Pennsylvania, Lewis Schmidt gives quartermaster records from the period the unit served in the Tortugas that list regular sales of one- or two-gallon quantities of whiskey to officers. The army was known to have a culture of hard drinking that had been aggravated by the war and the boredom of serving at an isolated location.

It is difficult to establish the period that Samuel Arnold is referring to in his allegations against the officers of the Fifth U.S. Artillery. The context suggests that it was probably following the arrival of 224 new recruits from Carlisle Barracks, Pennsylvania, in mid-May 1866. Arnold recalled: "Drunkenness ran riot on the island. There was not a day passed but that officers could be seen under its influence as they staggered down the walk leading from their barracks to the sally-port of the fort. Gaze where you would, the eye would come in contact with some of them, inebriated, a disgrace and dishonor to the service of the country which they represented."[12]

To what extent this described behavior during off-duty hours cannot be determined; it is difficult to imagine a regular army officer like Brigadier General Hill tolerating any hint of drunkenness among men on duty. But the facts about whiskey sales to officers speak for themselves. Arnold's bias and tendency toward lurid exaggerations should also be borne in mind. He was the man who had admitted under oath his complicity in Booth's conspiracy to kidnap the president but who later told Captain George Crabb, when threatened with leg-irons, that "no act of my life had justly merited me to be imprisoned."[13] Even a civilian judge and jury, unbiased and in the possession of those facts in the days following Lincoln's assassination, probably would have disagreed.

Samuel Arnold's contention that alcohol abuse contributed to brutality in dealing with recruits and prisoners likely was accurate. In the two most notorious examples, however—one of which resulted the shooting of a prisoner while the other involved the brutal and prolonged abuse of another—both occurred only after the convicts had become irrationally drunk themselves. On both occasions, this had been with the complicity of their guards. Clearly both men should have been restrained until they were sober before punishment was imposed, but that was not part of the soldiers' standing orders in such cases at the time.

The arrival of more than two hundred recruits on May 15 placed a severe burden on the less than one hundred veteran soldiers of the Fifth U.S. Artillery, the majority of whom had no leadership experience. Two companies of the 82nd U.S. Colored Troops remained at Fort Jefferson, but the requirements from each company were burdensome: mounting a twenty-four-hour guard as well as providing soldiers as cooks, for work details, and, after the trainees' arrival, as drill instructors.. The 193 prisoners remaining in custody were also some of the worst cases, life terms predominating.

In addition to close order drill, military customs and courtesy, and the maintenance of individual clothing and equipment, the new soldiers had to become proficient quickly on heavy artillery drills. Among other tasks, this involved hauling cannonballs from the lower shot cellars to the guns. For the heavier cannons on the third tier, the solid balls weighed 128 pounds. In large part, this explains why every infraction of the rules was punished by "carrying the ball," an effort to improve the recruits' physical condition. If the artillerymen failed physically in this regard, the guns would fall silent in the midst of an enemy attack. The black soldiers of the 82nd were not involved in the artillery training.

Another typical complaint of trainees was the quality and quantity of their rations. Arnold related that they would beg food while on guard. The prisoners received funds from friends and relatives and purchased much of their food from the sutler. This was usually not an option open to the new soldiers, who arrived in May and were probably not paid their first wages until October 1866. Punishments were not limited to duty days; "Sunday morning would always find 20 or 30 packing balls at the guardhouse in the boiling sun until some of them, exhausted and overcome by the heat, would fall in an almost lifeless condition and lie there . . . [later to be] picked up and conveyed to the hospital for medical treatment." Arnold also records a veteran artilleryman named Wheeler of Battery M who endured the punishment for thirty days, two hours on and two off, with no sign of ill effect.[14]

If the soldiers were injured or became ill, the determination of fitness for duty had to be made by the Fifth Artillery surgeon, Dr. John Bell. Soldiers often feigned illness, a practice called malingering by the laws of war, which subjected them to punishment. In cases of a difficult diagnosis or an unconvincing performance, Dr. Bell probably erred in favor of the command, believing that if soldiers were actually suffering from an acute illness or injury, they would return to sick call the next morning. The prisoners were usually treated by Dr. Holder, surgeon for the engineers, since they were technically employed by that department. As a group, the convicts were sicklier and poorly nourished and were more likely to be excused from heavy labor. This fairness, in part, may have contributed to the high regard felt by the prisoners for Dr. Holder.

The high level of disease continued as temperatures increased. Forty-four soldiers were listed as hospitalized. Privates James Berry and David W. May of Company I, Fifth Artillery, both died in June. By that summer the majority of the remaining prisoners were African-Americans. Dr. Mudd wrote on June 24: "There are about one hundred and seventy prisoners here at this time; out of this number there are not more than thirty whites." Construction on the fort had nearly stopped that summer, and the majority of the workers from the North had returned home. The last of the black soldiers at the Tortugas were reassigned to Fort Barrancas, Florida, on August 22, 1866. The monthly return noted that a prisoner named Bell Scott, formerly of the 96th U.S. Colored Infantry, Company I, had drowned, but no details of the incident remain.[15]

The new year of 1867 began quietly with a diminished number of prisoners on Garden Key. By the end of the month only fifty-six remained incarcerated. The weather was uncharacteristically cold, but by mid-January it was "growing warm and uncomfortable. We have a garden in the center of the Fort, the soil or surface of which has been brought from the mainland. It is now luxuriant with all kinds of vegetables that have been planted—beets, peas, tomatoes, beans, radishes, etc. The few trees we have never lose their foliage and the cocoanut, the only tree bearing, always with its peculiar fruit. The flowers that are cultivated are always in bloom."[16] The guardian of the flourishing garden plot was none other than Colonel Grenfell, whose sentence at "hard labor" was evidently being generously interpreted at the time. General Hill wrote to Grenfell's sister in May 1866: "He seems to be in vigorous health and cheerful. His employment, which is of his own seeking, is the charge of a small garden, in which he takes great interest."[17]

An incident that brought the Tortugas to national attention involved the mistreatment of a prisoner named James Dunn. On August 10, 1866, Dunn was among a number of convicts who had been tasked with unloading quartermaster and commissary supplies from two ships at the wharf. As the work proceeded Dunn and two of the guards were either provided with liquor by a member of the ship's crew or stole it from the commissary stores. Samuel Arnold recalled that Dunn "became beastly intoxicated."[18] He was apprehended as he reentered the fort, and the officer of the day was called. Brevet Major Charles C. MacConnell ordered that Dunn carry a ball as punishment, but it was soon clear that he was too drunk to do so. MacConnell then directed the sergeant to tie the prisoner to the bell post in front of the guardhouse. Ropes were tied around his wrists and he was suspended from the post. Dunn soon lost consciousness.

When Arnold returned to his quarters at 5:30 p.m. the prisoner had been moved from the post and was tied by his thumbs to an iron railing. He was still in a state of "drunken insensibility . . . the whole weight of his body resting upon his thumbs [which were] fearfully swollen and puffed out."[19] Dunn's ordeal was briefly interrupted when General Hill happened by and ordered him to be taken down and placed in the guardhouse. Several hours later Major MacConnell returned and ordered the sergeant to resume his punishment. Due to the injuries to his hands Dunn was incapable of carrying a ball and was again tied up by the wrists, a process that caused him to scream out in pain. The sounds of turmoil were so piercing that Captain

Benner, the lighthouse keeper, complained to MacConnell, who then had the guards gag Dunn with a bayonet. When the guard changed the next morning Dunn was taken to the hospital, where he remained until his release from imprisonment in November.[20]

Colonel George St. Leger Grenfell, despairing of the efforts of relatives and of the British government to secure his release, sent an inflammatory account of the mistreatment of prisoners and soldiers to Bradley T. Johnson of Richmond, Virginia. His motive was, at least in part, vindictiveness toward the officers of the Fifth Artillery. Johnson, a Confederate veteran, was quite sympathetic to Grenfell's plight. At his request, Johnson forwarded the allegations to an anti-administration newspaper. He wrote to Grenfell: "I at once have sent it to the [New York] World with a note becoming responsible for the Statements and asking its immediate publication."[21] The piece was published in the New York *World* on November 1, 1866, under the headline "From the Dry Tortugas: Revolting Treatment of Prisoners and Private Soldiers by the Military Authorities." Dunn's torment, the truth of which was certainly bad enough, was embellished by the outright lie that "the result of his punishment is the loss of his right thumb and his left hand."[22]

The treatment of another prisoner, John (or Frederick) Brown, was also distorted in the telling. Major Rittenhouse, while officer of the day, questioned Brown as to why Dr. Holder had excused him from duty. Brown made some equivocal answer, and the major returned him to the doctor to be examined. On a second examination, Brown was declared to be fit for duty. Rittenhouse ordered him to go to work, and Brown refused. When ordered to carry a ball as punishment, he refused that as well. "This was reported to General Hill, who ordered his hands to be tied behind his back, and that he should be thrown off the wharf into the water, and kept there until he offered to comply to the officer's terms."[23] Dunking in the harbor was an accepted punishment for convicts who refused to work. After being submerged for about two minutes Brown was pulled up and indicated that he would carry the ball. In a later sworn statement, Major Rittenhouse stated that Brown had shown no further illness and had not missed a day's work since. The newspaper account inaccurately stated that "on the 11th of September he was ordered to carry a shot for some pretended breach of discipline, and did so for a few hours, while suffering from an attack of diarrhea, and then finally refused to carry it longer."[24]

The article in the *World* also had a number of allegations regarding the mistreatment of soldiers and the recent recruits. All were probably based on some kernel of truth but were seriously exaggerated. A copy of the paper along with an emotional plea for an investigation soon found its way to the desk of President Johnson from an anonymous source. He referred the matter to the secretary of war, who ordered an inquiry by the district commander, Major General Philip Sheridan. When word of the publication reached Fort Jefferson a search by the provost marshal soon discovered a verbatim copy of the account among Colonel Grenfell's papers. He was ordered to solitary confinement and forbidden any books, papers, or writing materials.[25]

Brevet Lieutenant Colonel George L. Gillespie was sent to Garden Key by General Sheridan to head the investigation. In general Gillespie's report downplayed the severity of all of the instances of abuse. A number of those who should have been principal witnesses were not interviewed.[26] Samuel Arnold summed up his impression: "The investigation was a farce. Parties desiring to lay complaint were denied speech with the officer, and others were fearful of opening their lips for fear of after consequences."[27] At the War Department the adjutant general also seemed to have perceived the report as a whitewash.

After reviewing Brevet Lieutenant Colonel George L. Gillespie's report on the abuse of prisoners at Fort Jefferson, the adjutant general of the army directed General Hill to initiate court-martial proceedings against both Brevet Major Charles MacConnell and Brevet Major Benjamin F. Rittenhouse for the cruel treatment afforded James Dunn and Frederick Brown.[28] In the case of Major Charles MacConnell, the court-martial resulted in a written reprimand from Brigadier General Hill for tying up Dunn. MacConnell was "subsequently arrested and confined . . . to his quarters for several days." Hill was convinced that MacConnell's orders to the guard to tie up an unconscious man by his hands and thumbs demonstrated poor judgment and had the potential to cause serious harm. Major Rittenhouse presented a much more difficult case to prosecute. In his statement to the investigating officer, Rittenhouse had said: "Where there are so many prisoners confined for rape, arson, murder, &c it is fair to suppose that their rebellious and wicked dispositions may need cooling down occasionally when they see fit to resist the authority of their keepers."[29]

Brigadier General Hill did his best to draw up charges against Rittenhouse but finally could not justify punishment in a case that so clearly involved actions necessary to maintain authority and discipline over the prison population. Hill finally forwarded a letter to the War Department through his superior Major General P. H. Sheridan recommending that

Rittenhouse not be tried. Both Sheridan and the adjutant general agreed, and the order for the court-martial was recalled by the secretary of war on March 29, 1867.[30]

As the summer of 1867 dragged on, temperatures rose and tempers flared. In reality the lives and conditions endured by the soldiers were little better than those of the convicts. This situation often led to animosity toward the prisoners by their guards. An incident aggravating this hostility took place shortly after the assignment of Major George P. Andrews as commandant in June 1867. James Orr, a prisoner with a violent reputation, attacked the assistant quartermaster, George T. Jackson, stabbing him in the face in an attempt to cut his throat. Soon after the incident Major Andrews authorized Special Order no. 78, dated June 11, 1867. Paragraph three was a clear statement to the guards that the commandant had issued what amounted to "shoot to kill" orders, which included the statement "no sentinel who faithfully tries to do his duty shall ever see the inside of the guardhouse." Needless to say, the order received a great deal of attention and inspired widespread fear among the detainees.[31] In his memoirs Samuel Arnold repeated allegations that the draconian order originated with Secretary of War Stanton, but one probably does not have to look beyond the increased level of prisoner violence for its genesis.

Special Order no. 78 had only one victim, Private John Winters, alias Lee, formerly of the 17th U.S. Infantry, Company G, imprisoned for desertion. The 17th had been a recently reorganized regular army unit when it was stationed in Galveston, Texas, during the summer of 1866. The unit quickly gained a reputation for drunkenness, violence, and insubordination. The 17th Infantry had disgraced itself so badly that one pro-Union Galveston newspaper believed occupation by black troops would be preferable to that unit.[32] Winters had obtained liquor from one of the soldiers and was later described as "in a state of intoxication bordering on insanity." Dr. Mudd described the incident in a letter to his wife. "On the 31st of July, one of the prisoners being crazy drunk, noisy, and a little unruly, was shot and killed by one of the sentries. Instead of meeting with rebuke, the soldier was commended for his conduct. . . . [Winters] was a very orderly disposed man, nothing criminal about him." Arnold related that Winters was taken to the hospital and died within half an hour. He alleged that there was celebration when news of the shooting arrived at headquarters.[33]

As the intense heat continued in August, ominous evidence of yellow fever began be a matter of concern at Garden Key. It was later related that Captain George W. Crabb of the Fifth Artillery, who had recently returned from Cuba, had displayed symptoms of the disease but had recovered. Dr. Mudd, unaware of Crabb's exposure, incorrectly mentioned to his wife on August 25, "I am very well, though the island is becoming sickly. We have had one case of yellow fever here since I last wrote, which proved fatal. It originated here, and was not imported. . . . We have a Dr. Smith attending the Post . . . he has manifested a kind feeling toward me." The next day he continued, "Since I wrote yesterday, another case of fever has been admitted to the hospital, which from present symptoms, will likely prove fatal."[34] The epidemic had begun. The level of fear in that claustrophobic environment was intense. During an earlier epidemic Emily Holder wrote: "One day we had to acknowledge that the yellow fever had come; how we knew not; only the 'break-bone' fever, seemingly its first cousin, grew worse and worse, until it finally merged into genuine yellow fever. There were five deaths only, in these sad days that oppressed us like a nightmare."[35]

One of the perennial ailments that seems to have struck the post nearly every summer was the "break-bone" fever. "We have a disease here which is termed bone fever, or mild yellow fever, which has attacked at least three-fourths of the inmates of the Fort. It lasts generally but two or three days; during that time, the patient imagines every bone will break from the enormous pain he suffers in his limbs. None have died with it." This disease is in fact caused by a virus transmitted by mosquitoes of the same genus as those that carry yellow fever, the *Aedes* mosquitoes. It is known to modern medicine as dengue fever, and outbreaks occurred in Puerto Rico and Cuba as recently as the 1960s. While dengue fever is not usually fatal, full recovery from infections in individuals suffering from malnutrition or with compromised immunity often took weeks. The first known outbreak at Fort Jefferson was mentioned in 1862 and was repeated nearly every year subsequently.[36]

Among the first victims of the yellow fever was Dr. (Brevet Major) Joseph Sim Smith, the Fifth Artillery's surgeon. Dr. Smith had been popular among the soldiers and prisoners and had a reputation for kind treatment and concern. Dr. Mudd, employed at that time in the hospital dispensary, treated him almost constantly during the three days Smith was bedridden. Following Dr. Smith's death, Mudd also treated the doctor's wife, who eventually recovered. It was soon apparent that the disease was rapidly becoming an epidemic, and for fear of contagion, none of the officers or their wives visited the Smiths during their illness. Two companies of soldiers were removed to the nearby islands to isolate them from the fever and escaped exposure to the disease. The remaining two companies were retained as guards and eventually suffered twenty-nine deaths among the officers and men.[37]

Mudd wrote to his brother-in-law on September 8 giving an account of the true state of affairs at the Tortugas. "Nearly every man now on the island is infected with the disease. The hospitals are all full, and the greatest consternation prevails. Dr. Whitehurst arrived last night from Key West. He will relieve me. The two days I have had the management of the hospital no deaths have occurred, and all have improved that were taken in time." At first those stricken with the fever were taken to a small hospital on one of the nearby keys, but Mudd was able to convince the commandant that this practice, involving a trip of over one mile in an open boat, produced no benefit. Writing to his wife on September 13, he admitted that in spite of his efforts and those of Dr. Whitehurst, "I cannot refrain from letting you share the gloom which surrounds this seeming God-forsaken isle. Although three-fourths of the garrison have been removed, the epidemic seems to increase with unabated fury."[38] One of the forty-seven remaining prisoners, a civilian named James Kelly, made good his escape on September 23 when virtually no guards were being posted.[39]

The fever continued to claim victims from an ever-diminishing number of survivors. All of the officers of the Fifth Artillery were incapacitated or showing symptoms of the disease. Major Valentine Stone's wife and Dr. Smith's three-year-old son Harry died. Samuel Arnold was recovering and conspirator Michael O'Laughlin was expected to do so, but he took a turn for the worse when a visitor gave an "account of the recent deaths, he became excited, [and] sank into a collapse." He later suffered convulsions and died on the morning of September 23. Dr. Mudd was approaching exhaustion, and Dr. Whitehurst, already slowed by age, was clearly becoming incapacitated. Four other victims were buried on East Key with Michael O'Laughlin later that day. The doctor commented: "No more respect is shown the dead, be he officer or soldier, than the putrid remains of a dead dog. The burial party are allowed a drink of whiskey both before and after the burying, which infuses a little more life in them. They move quickly, and in half an hour after a man dies, he is put in a coffin, nailed down, carried to a boat, rowed a mile to an adjacent island, the grave dug, covered up, and the party returned, in the best of humor, for their drinks."[40]

Already distraught over the death of his wife, Major Stone was determined that their only child would not fall victim to the fever. They left Fort Jefferson on September 21 bound for Key West and the north. Word returned with the quartermaster ship *Matchless* four days later that Stone had fallen ill at Key West and died. With him also died his promises to inform the War Department of Dr. Mudd's valuable services to the garrison during the epidemic. At the end of September Mudd reported: "The cases that come in now are of the most malignant form, which shows that the principle of the disease is still active. Colonel Grenfel is quite sick with the disease; he was taken yesterday. I will do all that is possible to save him. He has been acting as nurse upon many of the officers recently. . . . A Dr. [Edward] Thomas has been assigned to this Post as medical director, and will be here tomorrow. Dr. Whitehurst will leave immediately after his arrival."[41]

From all accounts Dr. Thomas did not make a significant contribution to the conditions prevailing on Garden Key. It was recalled that he disappeared into his quarters with a supply of liquor and made rare appearances at the hospital, where a few patients were still making a recovery. Samuel Arnold wrote that Dr. Mudd was confined in his quarters by fever for some time, attended only by himself and Edman Spangler—"during the entire period of his illness was never visited by the New York doctor, the surgeon in charge, he remaining closeted in his room." This reprehensible behavior was noted by many. A second prisoner, James Markey, died of yellow fever on October 1. By the latter days of October the situation was reversed; Dr. Thomas was stricken with fever and Mudd was able to assume his duties, which he was "beginning to find unpleasant."[42] The epidemic ended in mid-November as cooler winds began to blow in from the north.

In November 1867 following the terrors of the yellow fever outbreak, Dr. Holder's idyllic description of Fort Jefferson first appeared in print, providing his American readers with a description widely at variance with the prevailing realities.

> On entering the fort the stranger is surprised to see a pleasant parade-ground of fine Bermuda grass—the choicest of all lawn grasses—and large groups of evergreen mangroves and buttonwoods. Towering above all are the elegant plumes of the cocoa palm. A neat walk leads to the officers' quarters through an arching group of mangroves, flanked by long rows of ordnance material. And as we approach headquarters a beautiful group of mangroves is seen, furnished with shady seats and lounging places, where the ever acceptable hammock swings invitingly. . . . The veranda, hand-rail, pillars, and all festooned and draped with jasmines, Thunbergias, morning glories, and cypress vines.[43]

In fairness to Dr. Holder, he had left Garden Key before one could stand on the walls of Fort Jefferson and see nearby Bird Key pocked with graves and planted with whitewashed wooden crosses.

After nearly five and one-half years Major McFarland was finally relieved of his responsibilities at Forts Jefferson and Taylor in January 1868 by Lieutenant Colonel James H. Simpson. Simpson was a U.S. Military Academy graduate in 1832 and had briefly served as a colonel of volunteers in the Fourth New Jersey Volunteer Infantry during McClellan's Peninsula and Seven Days' campaigns around Richmond. He resumed his career with the engineers in August 1862 and had been promoted to lieutenant colonel as an officer of the regular army in June 1863.[44]

Simpson inherited a number of unresolved issues that were aggravated by the failure of Congress to fund construction at Fort Jefferson adequately during 1867–68. An investigation into the outbreak of yellow fever in the summer of 1867 was highly critical of the engineers' failure to resolve problems with sanitation and the general inadequacy of the facilities for the disposal of sewage. The investigation had also blamed the outbreak on rotting wood in several temporary structures maintained by the engineers on the parade. A more confrontational situation surrounded conflicting claims for permanent quarters from the officers of the Fifth Artillery and the engineers' civilian supervisors. This would culminate in the forced eviction of an engineer's family from quarters in May 1868 by Commandant Major Charles C. MacConnell, during which "a detail of soldiers pitched the family's furnishings out-of-doors."[45] Lieutenant Colonel Simpson inherited a number of problems not easily resolved.

The escape of Colonel George St. Leger Grenfell from Fort Jefferson in March 1868 gave evidence of long planning and preparation. The plot included two of the most disreputable convicts incarcerated there, the irrepressible J. W. Adare and James Orr, whose attempted murder of George Jackson had resulted in the "shoot to kill" orders in June 1867. The other two involved in the scheme were prisoner Joseph Holroyd, a convicted rapist from the Union First Louisiana Cavalry, and Private William Noreil of Battery I, Fifth U.S. Artillery. Even with the assistance of Private Noreil, the odds were very much against success. The four prisoners had to get out of locked casemates and evade their sentry. Oars, anchors, and rudders for the boats were normally kept locked in the guardhouse, and the small boats were secured at the wharf by a locked wooden boom. The night of the escape, March 6, 1868, Noreil would be manning the guard post by the boats for only two hours between eleven and one in the morning, but the weather conditions were terrible. Samuel Arnold recorded that a gale had been blowing from the north for the five previous days, and waves and whitecaps were evident even within the sheltered harbor.[46]

Colonel Grenfell may have had good reason to defy the odds and make the attempt. Brevet Major Charles MacConnell had assumed command of the fort days before, replacing Major George P. Andrews, who had been reassigned. MacConnell was understandably hostile to Grenfell, whose revelations of the torture of James Dunn while MacConnell had been officer of the day had led to his censure by court-martial. Upon assignment, MacConnell had relieved Grenfell of his gardening pursuits and ordered him to perform much more physically demanding duties. This may have been perceived by Grenfell as the prelude to even worse treatment in the future. In a remote environment commanded by an embittered enemy given to heavy drinking, nothing was impossible. The angry sea may suddenly have seemed a viable alternative.[47]

At some time after eleven on the night of March 6, with Noreil's assistance, the four prisoners escaped their quarters and gathered on Number One Wharf in driving cold rain, just outside the only entrance to Fort Jefferson. If they could navigate the reefs and shoals surrounding Garden Key, the north wind would drive them south toward Havana and freedom. The fishing smack belonging to Noreil's Battery I was lifted half out of the anchorage and dragged over the locked boom into the harbor. Stowing their scant supplies in the boat, they boarded and began pulling on the oars. By the time the sergeant of the guard was informed that the guard at that post did not answer, Grenfell and his companions had disappeared into the darkness and the wind-driven rain.[48]

When the alarm was raised at midnight on March 7, it was soon discovered that Private Noreil and four convicts were missing, along with the boat belonging to Battery I. No pursuit was launched, however, since the officers were convinced that the five "must have been swept into eternity before they were three hundred yards from the fort."[49] A coast guard vessel that had ridden out the storm in the harbor was pressed into service to begin a search for the fugitives the next morning. Captain Slott of the *Bibb* did not hold much hope of finding them but sailed all day to the south and southeast without finding a trace of the men or the boat. Given the intensity of the previous night's storm, he believed that it would have been impossible for a small, heavily loaded vessel to have survived in the open sea.[50]

Weeks passed and no information concerning the fate of the escapees was received. Inquiries were sent to authorities in Havana but with negative results. An investigation by Lieutenant Paul Roemer also produced few results other than concluding that Colonel Grenfell had probably received funds in an unopened registered letter and that these had likely been used in part to bribe Private Noreil. The War Department later concluded that Grenfell and his companions had perished in the storm.[51] In an ironic turn of events the next month, Grenfell's garden, in the past always sterile and unproductive in spite of all his efforts, suddenly became a success. Dr. Mudd told his wife: "There are a great quantity of ripe tomatoes, peas, beans, and 'collards' in the garden, now suitable for table use. The corn is in silk, and soon there will be roasting ears."[52]

Two companies of the Fifth Artillery that had temporarily been stationed in New Orleans due to unrest caused by the Military Reconstruction Act returned to Fort Jefferson in early May. Lieutenant Colonel E. C. Bainbridge briefly took command from Major MacConnell on May 4 but was relived by Brigadier General Hill five days later. A report of the questionable conduct of assistant surgeon Dr. Edward Thomas during the yellow fever epidemic in the fall of 1867 had evidently reached the office of the army surgeon general. Thomas's contract was annulled on April 18, 1868; he was relieved of his duties and left on May 15. He was replaced by another civilian under contract, Dr. William E. Day, who arrived on May 12.[53]

By late 1867 and early 1868 resistance to military occupation and Reconstruction was growing in many areas of the South. Attacks against Republican political figures—often recent arrivals from the North, or "carpetbaggers"—became more frequent. Freed slaves who tried to exercise their newly won civil rights were targets of threats and intimidation. An incident in rural Greene County, Alabama, gained widespread attention when federal military authorities decided to make examples of its perpetrators. The case was not particularly violent, nor did it approach the level of criminal activity by local Democrats that was becoming common in many communities.

Among the most unpopular recent converts to radical Republicanism in Greene County was a farmer and Methodist minister, Joseph B. F. Hill. Hill had joined the Union League and served as a prominent local supporter of congressional Reconstruction as well as leading a school for freedmen. On March 14, 1868, Hill was conducting some business in Eutaw, Alabama, when he was confronted by young William Pettigrew. The altercation was said to have been over a sixty-dollar debt for a quantity of firewood purchased by Hill from Pettigrew's father. The loud disagreement soon came to blows by Pettigrew and drew a large crowd of the younger man's supporters.

Reverend Hill was repeatedly struck and threatened by the cheering crowd and was saved from being ridden out of town on a rail only by the arrival of James Clarke, Eutaw's chancellor. The bloodied Hill was then permitted to leave and rode the ten miles north to his home in Union, Alabama.[54]

That evening Hill was first visited by James Steele, one of the mob who had assaulted him. "Claiming to represent Greene County whites, he warned Hill to leave the county, citing Hill's unpopular Republican activities as justification." Later a larger group of five young men arrived and threatened him to be gone within three days or "expect the worst." Two of the night riders "denounced his 'damned Radicalism' and informed Hill that 'no niggers should ever be educated to vote again in Greene County.'" Clearly believing the seriousness of the threat, Reverend Hill quickly departed the county.[55]

The obvious political overtones of the case probably explain why federal military authorities seized on it to demonstrate the power of the military government that had been established as a result of the Reconstruction Act of March 2, 1867. Ultimate authority rested with the Third Military District of Alabama, Georgia, and Florida, commanded by General George G. Meade. Joseph Hill filed a formal complaint with a nearby office of the Bureau of Refugees, Freedmen and Abandoned Lands, or Freedmen's Bureau, detailing the incident and providing the names of the offenders. In response, military authorities issued arrest warrants that were served in Eutaw against fifteen of the accused by a company of cavalry. Meade believed that it would be impossible to secure convictions in civilian court in Greene County and that the only viable option was trial before a military tribunal. Initial plans called for a trial in Montgomery, Alabama, but following the release of the accused on bond, the venue was moved to Selma.

The trial before a four-man military commission opened on April 16 at army headquarters in Selma. The accused were charged with one or more counts of "riot," "assault and battery," and "lynching." The lynching charge under Alabama law was not limited to the taking of life but included "any attempt to force an individual from an area." As the trial began, the attorneys for the defense, Eutaw residents John J. Jolly and John G. Pierce, unsuccessfully challenged the jurisdiction of federal military authorities. That was in spite of a decision of the U.S. Supreme Court in 1866 entitled *Ex parte Milligan* that had declared military trials unconstitutional in areas where civil courts were functional. One of the stranger aspects of the trial was the absence of the accuser, Joseph B. F. Hill. One likely explanation could be traced to the vicious attacks on his character in the predominantly

Democratic press in Alabama. Accusations against Hill ranged from his having been expelled from the Methodist Church for theft to being a "miserable scallawag" or a man of "no character" and the suggestion that at some point he had stolen the coffin of a Union soldier.[56]

The trial was concluded on the second day. Several credible witnesses to the confrontation in Eutaw did testify; however, the threats to Hill later that night at his home in Union, Alabama, were supported only by Hill's son, Soule Hill. A number of witnesses "attempted to establish that Soule Hill could not be trusted to tell the truth even under oath." The defendants remained confined in the town jail in Selma as ten days passed before the verdict was announced. In General Orders 72, Meade's Third Military District headquarters sentenced defendants John Cullen, Frank Mundy, Samuel Strayhorn, and Hugh White to one year's hard labor. William Pettigrew, Thomas Roberts, and James Steele were sentenced to two years' hard labor. All sentences were to be carried out "immediately at Fort Jefferson in the Dry Tortugas Islands." The press expressed shock and outrage at the severity of the punishments for offenses that in a civil district court would normally have resulted in fines or a short jail sentence.[57]

After the sentence was announced, those convicted were placed in chains and quickly transported to their destination. The intended secrecy of the operation was repeatedly compromised, and many Democratic newspapers expressed outrage at the treatment of the "young gentlemen." After arriving at Garden Key on May 18 they were described by Lincoln conspirator Samuel Arnold as having been convicted of "the alleged offence of threatening to ride a carpet-bagger on a rail. On them was centered a deep hatred and prejudice. They were termed Ku-Klux by the provost marshal for the purpose of engendering hatred in the hearts of the soldiers against them, in which it failed to some extent." Arnold's paranoia concerning the "dark motives" of the officers serving at Fort Jefferson colors many of his later accounts. He concluded: "Their manner of treatment was cruel, unjust, and tyrannical in the extreme."[58] In a letter to his wife, Dr. Mudd also glosses over the "Eutaw Prisoners" conviction for what amounted to political terrorism: "Their offense hardly amounted to a breach of the peace."[59]

Widespread support for the young men grew in the meantime in the press and among reputable segments of the southern population. Appeals to General Meade for clemency were soon successful. He informed the men's defense attorneys of his intentions on May 17, 1868. Third Military District General Order 80 pardoned the men but also made clear that in the future such offenses would not be tolerated. "Contributing also to his decision, he explained, was the suffering caused the prisoners' families and the promises of future exemplary conduct. He further mentioned that had Greene County officials not ignored previous crimes, the men might not have assaulted Hill. . . . Meade promised that criminals could expect no special consideration or clemency in the future." The seven prisoners were released from Fort Jefferson on June 12, 1868, having served less than one month of their sentences.[60]

At the time he mentioned the prisoners from Alabama, Dr. Mudd was neglecting writing to his wife because of the behavior of the acting provost marshal. Mudd described him as "an inquisitive and officious Yankee, from away down in Maine. He is one of those officious individuals fond of ruling, considering himself one of the elect, and adds daily new rules for the government of the prisoners, which tend to be more despotic than the laws of the ancient barbarians. All letters are carefully perused by him, not as a duty of his office, but because of his prying spirit and disposition to meddle." In his next letter, dated June 11, 1868, Dr. Mudd noted: "This letter goes out by one of the seven men recently . . . released, [they] leave to-day for their homes."[61]

Although the engineers had completed permanent sanitary facilities and sewers beneath the parade by the summer of 1868, the conditions were not significantly improved. Mudd commented that "the atmosphere around the Fort, owing to the filthy condition of the moat outside, is terribly offensive at times and bids fair to breed another pestilence." Most at the time believed that tropical diseases were caused by "miasma" or vapors generated by decay and stagnant water. The discovery by Dr. Walter Reed that the ever-present mosquitoes were the carriers of yellow fever was still thirty years in the future. Due to repeated complaints the engineers began excavating the moat to its full depth and disposing of the offending materials in the bay as June continued predictably hot and humid.[62]

July 1868 marked the end of the third year that Samuel Arnold, Edman Spangler, and Dr. Samuel Mudd had endured in the Tortugas. An attempt by Mudd to secure his freedom through a writ of *habeas corpus* at federal court in Key West had failed. The U.S. Supreme Court, threatened by powerful radicals in Congress, refused to accept jurisdiction of any cases involving Reconstruction for over two years. The attempted removal of Secretary of War Edwin Stanton, the man many characterized as the force behind the prosecution of the Lincoln conspirators, led to the attempted impeachment of the president. Andrew Johnson survived that threat in April and May 1868, and a presidential pardon for the three remaining prisoners in the waning months of his administration was a real possibility. Following the election of Ulysses S. Grant in November 1868, Frances Mudd wrote to her husband from Baltimore, Maryland: "I truly believe Johnson will release you before he goes out of office; and if he does not, I have assurance Grant will, so for my sake bear up a while longer, and God will send you safely home to me and our dear little children."[63]

The Fortress Abandoned

1869–1874

The size and isolation of Fort Jefferson often resulted in very different experiences than those of soldiers stationed at typical military installations. In part this was due to the lack of any neighboring civilian communities as well as the unusual mix of a military garrison, immigrant civilian workers, convicts, political prisoners, and transient fishermen. The role of the Tortugas in national defense policy also had a strong impact on its perceived importance. The age of expansion and Manifest Destiny culminating in the Mexican Cession ended before the foundations of Fort Jefferson had risen more than a few feet above high tide. The extreme sectional tensions and political gridlock of the 1850s prevented extension of American slavery into the Gulf, Cuba, and Central America—otherwise a real possibility. Such an extension would have placed the Tortugas firmly in the strategic role many had predicted for it as the "key to the Gulf." That was not to be; the eve of the American Civil War found Garden Key still without garrison or guns.

Despite the war with Mexico and tensions with Spain, until the secession crisis of 1860–61 the pace of life on Garden Key was measured and similar to that of the remainder of the antebellum South. Slavery was never noted for producing a highly motivated work force, although slaves eventually performed the heaviest and most demanding labor. The white workforce, skilled and unskilled, was often reported as functioning at about half the efficiency one would expect in a temperate climate. Tropical fevers and injuries slowed construction, as did the unwillingness of workers from the North to remain through the summer months. Engineer supervisors and professionals often took advantage of labor and funding shortages to make extended social calls to Key West or Havana.

One strong similarity existed between service at Garden Key and the outposts of the distant West: an almost total lack of supervision and tours of inspection by officials from Washington prior to the outbreak of war. Chief of Engineers Joseph Totten made only one visit to Fort Jefferson in 1855 in conjunction with naturalist Louis Agassiz. That brief tour was probably done more at the behest of the Smithsonian Institution than of the War Department. Another factor in common with western outposts was the extreme slowness and unpredictability of official mail service. Delays gave commanders of remote sites much greater latitude in decision making than those nearer regional headquarters.

A shortcoming Garden Key shared with all remote sites in the military was the lack of women and children. Primitive or inadequate housing was often the primary cause. Other considerations were the cost of expensive preserved food and the lack of educational opportunity. The threats of enemy attack and epidemic diseases remained real in many locations. Before the spring of 1860, however, Fort Jefferson was blessed with a lively community of dependants. Dr. Joseph Holder and his wife Emily had arrived in 1859 with their son Charles. Captain Daniel Woodbury, the superintending engineer, resided in the partially completed officer quarters with his wife and five children. Outside the walls in the workers' quarters a number of slave families lived alongside the engineer cook, Mrs. Fogarty, and her children and the family of Mr. Phillips, the overseer. Wives conducted classes for the children, and Dr. Holder often took a number of the older boys out on the reef and to neighboring islands to collect specimens and for lessons in marine biology. For a time Mrs. Woodbury conducted music lessons for the girls.

A dissenting summary of nineteenth-century life at Fort Jefferson and on Garden Key was written by one whose long residence there also qualified him to render a final farewell: "I have endeavored to give some idea of this out-of-the-world fortress and its surroundings. Strangers landing here for a few hours, no doubt, may indulge in rhapsodies about its beauty, its few cocoanut trees, just like those in pictures that adorn little missionary tracts, its apocryphal banana trees, its luxuriant grass and evergreen foliage; but perhaps if they were doomed to a three years' residence on this barren, broiling, coral island, their ideas would be considerably modified, and a good deal of the rosy tinting bleached out of their pictures."[1]

Following the death of General Totten in 1864 and the retirement of Richard Delafield in 1866 the entire range of seacoast fortifications witnessed drastic declines in congressional funding. In 1868 forts with major ongoing construction were cut to a uniform $50,000. The fiscal year 1869 budget appropriated by Congress failed to provide any funding for Fort Jefferson. By the time the garrison was withdrawn from Garden Key in 1874

Figure 22. View of the 1876 lighthouse atop bastion C, with a 15-inch Rodman in the foreground. Photo by Paulien Reid.

many facilities had to be turned over to caretakers. The appropriation for the Fortifications Bill that year declined to $624,000, the lowest in nearly twenty years. The reasons for changed priorities are not difficult to trace. That same year the Pensions Bill, primarily for Civil War veterans, rose to $29 million. Enforcement of the Reconstruction Act in the South and the defense of increasingly politically powerful western states against the Indian threat consumed an additional $33 million.[2]

The year 1869 would bring many major changes to Garden Key. Lieutenant Colonel Simpson was reassigned as superintending engineer of the defenses of Baltimore harbor.[3] He was replaced by Lieutenant Colonel Charles E. Blunt. The battalion of the Fifth U.S. Artillery was relieved by four batteries of the Third U.S. Artillery, who departed Fort Warren, Massachusetts, aboard the steamship *Rapidan* and arrived at Fort Jefferson on February 25, 1869.[4] In his history of the Fifth Artillery, James C. Bush commented that the command was greatly cheered by being relieved of their postwar duties. "During the reconstruction period our officers had their share of the onerous duties of that disagreeable time. It was with a sense of relief, therefore, that the regiment turned northward early in 1869 and took stations along the New England coast."[5]

THE FORTRESS ABANDONED: 1869–1874

Colonel Blunt soon discovered that no permanent arrangement had been made to provide regular transport and communication between Garden Key and Key West. Given the limited budget a charter was probably Blunt's only option. After discussions with knowledgeable residents of Key West and having received authorization from Chief of Engineers Humphreys, he considered the charter of the schooner *Oriental* for $575 per month. This proved unnecessary since lighthouse tenders were arriving at Garden and Loggerhead keys regularly at the time. The indication was that Congress would pass a Fortifications Bill to fund construction for fiscal year 1870, and if work was to be quickly resumed, dependable communication was imperative.[6]

The three surviving state prisoners, Samuel Arnold, Dr. Samuel Mudd, and Edman Spangler, were all pardoned by President Andrew Johnson in the waning days of his administration. The last to depart the Dry Tortugas was probably Edman Spangler, ironically the only one among them serving less than a life sentence.

In the postwar environment of straightened budgets the only construction progressing at Fort Jefferson was concerned with completing barracks and officers' quarters and improving the sanitary facilities, the engineers' most persistent failure. The primary sources of labor during 1869 and 1870 were workers from Key West and the remaining prisoners. On hand at both Fort Taylor and Fort Jefferson were great numbers of heavy guns and carriages that had not been mounted. Given the lack of funds, Commander of the Army General William T. Sherman ordered that the task be completed by the artillerymen assigned to the two posts. Blunt and the engineers assisted with hardware and requisitioned a number of structural items made necessary by the larger, more modern guns to be mounted on the third tier.

Engineer operations were closed down on June 30, 1870, as rumors of yellow fever became widespread at Key West. Lieutenant Colonel Blunt spent the next four months in New York arranging for artillery hardware to be shipped to Garden Key. During his absence the assistant engineer at Garden Key, Lieutenant Asa T. Abbott, departed aboard the quartermaster schooner *Matchless* the morning of October 19. By 4:00 p.m. gale force winds were lashing the Gulf. The schooner anchored that night ten miles off the Marquesas Keys; by morning the storm had become a hurricane. Mainly because of the experienced crew, the ship survived the storm despite extreme difficulties. She returned to Key West the afternoon of October 21

Figure 23. Detailed view of the plate-iron lighthouse constructed on bastion C in 1876. Photo by Paulien Reid.

and to Fort Jefferson the next morning. Abbott noted that nearly all the slate had been torn from the roof of the old officer quarters. Other damage included two wrecked government boats, extensive damage to the sutler's small yacht, wharfs destroyed, and twenty-five tons of coal stored outside the walls completely swept away.

After long neglect by Congress, a Fortifications Bill including Fort Jefferson for 1872 passed that body on November 22, 1871. Priorities for construction would be the officer quarters, the barracks, and the counterscarp or seawall. Learning at the end of April that work would resume, the post surgeon, Dr. Samuel A. Storrow, recommended that the return of the workmen be delayed until November 1872 to avoid wasteful delays caused by the quarantine then in effect. Colonel Blunt and General Humphries agreed, and Blunt remained in New York on temporary duty at the agency's headquarters.

Work progressed uninterrupted through November and December but a reordering of priorities was directed by Chief of Engineers Humphries in January due to increased tension with Great Britain when the Grant administration pressed the *Alabama* claims for damages to U.S. shipping by warships built in Britain for the Confederacy. Six massive 15-inch Rodman cannons and four 300-pounder Parrott guns were to be mounted on the barbette (third) tier. Each gun weighed in excess of 50,000 pounds, and their size required that they be hoisted from the parade fifty feet below. Following the completion of that task, post commander Major Romeyn B. Ayres requested that a major effort be made to complete the seawall. Without this barrier sandbars had formed that would eventually block the drains and sewers and aggravate problems with hygiene. Colonel Blunt agreed and received authorization to prioritize any portion still incomplete in June for renewed work in the autumn.

President Grant signed authorization on June 10, 1872, for the engineers to expend $42,500 on Garden Key in fiscal year 1873. Priorities were to complete the counterscarp, the 15-inch Rodman positions, one of the ammunition magazines, and the barracks. By April 1873 Blunt was finally able to report that the seawall was complete, and there was "now a clear and good circulation all around the fort."[7] By May 1, 1873, artisans from the North had departed and quarantine had been established (meaning a twelve-day period of isolation for arriving ships), leaving just a few workers who were natives of Key West to secure materials and complete minor projects.

A second major yellow fever outbreak in five years plagued Garden Key in August and September 1873. Surgeon Francis J. Gould had allowed his thirteen-year-old son Charles to accompany the quartermaster schooner *Matchless* on a brief supply and mail run to Key West as a vacation from the monotony of late summer at Fort Jefferson. Spending four days there, Charles ambled around the wharves observing the loading and unloading of cattle, fruit, and fish. One bark, the Norwegian *Tonsberghus*, had just returned from Havana, where it had lost two crew members to yellow fever. The *Matchless* returned to the Tortugas on August 13. Charles felt unwell but did not mention his illness for three days, until he was unable to leave his bed. Dr. Gould diagnosed his son with "bilious remittent fever" and isolated him for a week, after which Charles visited friends in the enlisted barracks.[8]

A new assistant surgeon had just reported to Fort Jefferson after commissioning as a first lieutenant in June. Dr. Joseph Yates Porter, a native of Key West, had graduated from Jefferson Medical College in Philadelphia in 1870. In addition to his familiarity with the area and its health problems, Porter himself was a yellow fever survivor and had studied the disease extensively. Porter eventually served sixteen years on active duty, retiring as a lieutenant colonel. Following his separation, he became the health officer of the State of Florida, an office he held until 1917.[9]

Shortly after Dr. Porter's arrival yellow fever broke out at Garden Key on August 23, 1873. Gould and Porter, voluntarily assisted by Dr. Joseph Otto of Key West, eventually treated thirty-seven cases of the disease; fourteen people died. The healthy soldiers of the garrison were removed to Loggerhead Key, where they temporarily lived in tents. All four of Dr. Gould's young children were stricken but survived. Among the dead was Lieutenant James E. Bell, the commandant of Fort Jefferson. He was replaced by Captain Loomis Langdon, who had served with Major Arnold in 1861 at Garden Key when the post was first garrisoned.[10]

At the height of the outbreak on September 6 senior army surgeon Harvey E. Brown arrived. He took charge of the hospital as well as conducting a thorough inspection of the hygiene of the post for Captain Langdon. The sewers and sanitary facilities, as always, were defective, and the tidal flows failed to flush them out. Dr. Brown also found several temporary engineer structures both inside and outside the fort to be in a state of decay, one shed being filled with old lumber covered with fungus. Captain Langdon responded to the report by sending a scathing list of accusations against the Corps of Engineers to the Department Headquarters. In addition to bad plumbing and ramshackle mildewed sheds, Langdon reported that engineer employees defied regulations and buried garbage and allowed it to rot.[11]

The Tortugas were struck by another major hurricane on October 6 and 7, 1873. Both officer quarters and barracks suffered major damage to roofing, leading to a nearly complete flooding of the buildings. Windows were shattered and exterior blinds destroyed. A large latrine located outside the walls, completed in the winter of 1872–73, was entirely swept away by the storm surge and wind-driven waves. Nineteen cattle and an unknown number of mules penned in the nearby stable suffered the same fate. A bakery and brick oven on the parade were damaged to such an extent that they were rendered unserviceable. Patients in the post hospital had to be relocated when that structure lost its roof. Post commander Captain Langdon reported the destruction, and Colonel Blunt later estimated repair costs of $20,000. The soldiers could not continue to occupy the barracks due to dampness and the danger of falling plaster. As in the past, they were relocated into the second tier casemates. Only thirty-six habitable rooms remained in the officer quarters.[12]

Late that year a group of American filibusters attempted to aid revolutionaries in Cuba. The steamer *Virginius* was captured by Spanish authorities. Thirty-seven American citizens were subsequently executed at Santiago de Cuba for piracy. Calls for war with Spain immediately broke out in the United States. Colonel Blunt and other officers charged with arming fortifications in the Gulf were placed on alert and ordered to make all possible preparations. By December 1873 the War Department was notified that Fort Jefferson was ready for a large garrison if the situation made it necessary. The diplomatic crisis was later resolved when it was discovered that the ship belonged to Cuban revolutionaries and had been illegally registered as a U.S. vessel. Spain released the surviving members of the expedition and paid $80,000 in indemnity to the families of the Americans executed.[13]

Because of the hurricane damage at Fort Jefferson and the ongoing threat of yellow fever the Department of the South recommended to Commander of the Army William T. Sherman that the garrison be relocated to Fort Barrancas, Florida, and that Fort Jefferson be transferred to the Corps of Engineers for repair and completion. Sherman recommended approval of the action to Secretary of War William W. Belknap. President Grant gave permission to transfer the soldiers in November 1873. Captain Langdon left the Tortugas for Fort Barrancas on November 19. The remainder of the company relocated on January 11, 1874, leaving the armaments and ammunition in the care of Ordnance Sergeant Adolph Dangerfield and a small detail of privates.[14] Responsibility for engineer operations was transferred on January 1, 1874, when Captain Jared A. Smith replaced Colonel Blunt as superintending engineer for Forts Taylor and Jefferson.

Following the removal of the garrison in January 1874, funding was nearly eliminated and was sufficient for little more than to hire caretakers to secure engineer property. This cut in funding was symptomatic of budget reductions for all seacoast facilities. As noted, the entire allocation for fortifications for fiscal year 1874 was only $624,000.[15] A small detail of soldiers remained at Fort Jefferson to maintain the guns and ammunition. In 1889 the post was transferred to the Marine Hospital Service for use as a station to isolate vessels in quarantine. Tensions building with Spain in 1898 led to the stationing of a garrison of the Fifth U.S. Artillery there for a time. The navy used the facility as a coaling station and rendezvous for warships on patrol around Cuba. The U.S.S. *Maine* loaded coal from the facility before its fateful journey to anchor in Havana harbor. The night of February 15, 1898, the *Maine* was destroyed by a mysterious explosion that triggered the Spanish-American War. During World War I the Garden Key lighthouse was decomissioned. The post was the site of a wireless station and the harbor included a primitive facility for naval seaplanes. The end of the war in 1918 marked the beginning of a seventeen-year period of neglect. President Franklin D. Roosevelt rescued Fort Jefferson from further deterioration on January 4, 1935, when it was declared a national monument.[16] It would become the Dry Tortugas National Park on October 26, 1992.

The days of intensive occupation and exploitation of the Dry Tortugas are past. Fort Jefferson endures, partially in ruins, but the surrounding environment has made a remarkable recovery. The seabird nesting colony on Bush Key witnesses the return of an estimated 100,000 sooty terns each year. Although threatened worldwide, green, hawksbill, and loggerhead turtles still dig nests and lay eggs in the white sands of the keys. Forests of living coral in the clear shallow waters shelter colorful reef fishes as well as predatory sharks and barracuda. Credit for the good stewardship and preservation of the park belongs to the rangers of the National Park Service. Now Garden Key's only permanent residents, rangers guided and assisted tens of thousands of visitors in past years and weathered three major hurricanes in 2005 alone. As history teaches, nature often shows its claws in the Dry Tortugas.

THE FORTRESS ABANDONED: 1869–1874

APPENDIX A

Fort Jefferson's Superintending Engineers

Captain Horatio G. Wright / Dec. 1846–Mar. 1856
U.S. Military Academy, Class of 1841

Captain Daniel P. Woodbury / Mar. 1856–Nov. 1860
U.S. Military Academy, Class of 1836

Captain Montgomery C. Meigs / Nov. 1860–Feb. 1861
U.S. Military Academy, Class of 1836

Captain James St. Clair Morton / Feb. 1861–Mar. 1862
U.S. Military Academy, Class of 1851

Major Walter McFarland / Mar. 1862–Jan. 1868
U.S. Military Academy, Class of 1860

Lieutenant Colonel James H. Simpson / Jan. 1868–Jan. 1869
U.S. Military Academy, Class of 1832

Lieutenant Colonel Charles E. Blunt / Jan. 1869–Dec. 1873
U.S. Military Academy, Class of 1846

Major Jared A. Smith / Jan. 1874–Dec. 1876
U.S. Military Academy, Class of 1862

APPENDIX B

Fort Jefferson's Commanding Officers

Maj. Lewis Golding Arnold
2nd U.S. Artillery / Jan. 1861–Sept. 1861

Lieut. Col. Horace Brooks
2nd U.S. Artillery / Sept. 1861–Mar. 1862

Col. Haldimand S. Putnam
7th New Hampshire Volunteers / Mar. 1862–Jun. 1862

Lieut. Col. Louis W. Tinelli
90th New York Volunteers / Jun. 1862–Dec. 1862

Lieut. Col. George W. Alexander
47th Pennsylvania Volunteers / Dec. 1862–Mar. 1864

Col. Charles Hamilton
110th New York Volunteers / Mar. 1864–May 1865

Capt. James Doyle
110th New York Volunteers / Jun. 1865–Jun. 1865

Maj. Henry C. Devendorf
110th New York Volunteers / Jul. 1865–Aug. 1865

Capt. William R. Prentice
161st New York Volunteers / Aug. 1865–Sept. 1865

Maj. George E. Wentworth
82nd U.S. Colored Troops / Sept. 1865–Nov. 1865

Bvt. Brig. Gen. Bennett H. Hill
5th U.S. Artillery / Nov. 1865–Jun. 1867

Maj. George P. Andrews
5th U.S. Artillery / Jun. 1867–Jul. 1867

Maj. Valentine H. Stone
5th U.S. Artillery / Jul. 1867–Sept. 1867

Maj. George P. Andrews
5th U.S. Artillery / Sept. 1867–Mar. 1868

Bvt. Maj. Charles C. MacConnell
5th U.S. Artillery / Mar. 1868–May 1868

Lieut. Col. E. C. Bainbridge
5th U.S. Artillery / May 1868

Bvt. Brig. Gen. Bennett H. Hill
5th U.S. Artillery / May 1868–Jan. 1869

Lieut. Col. Henry J. Hunt
3rd U.S. Artillery / Feb. 1869–Mar. 1869

Capt. John Edwards
3rd U.S. Artillery / Apr. 1869

Lieut. Col. Augustus A. Gibson
3rd U.S. Artillery / May 1869–Oct. 1870

Capt. Lorenzo Lorain
3rd U.S. Artillery / Nov. 1870–Jan. 1871

1st Lieut. James M. Lancaster
3rd U.S. Artillery / Feb. 1871–Mar. 1871

Maj. Romeyn B. Ayres
3rd U.S. Artillery / Apr. 1871–Sept. 1871

Capt. Erskine Gittings
3rd U.S. Artillery / Oct. 1871–Aug. 1872

1st Lieut. Abraham Verplanck
3rd U.S. Artillery / Sept. 1872–Oct. 1872

Capt. Loomis L. Langdon
1st U.S. Artillery, Co. M / Nov. 1872–June 1873

1st Lieut. James M. Ingalls
1st U.S. Artillery, Co. M / July 1873

1st Lieut. James E. Bell
1st U.S. Artillery, Co. M / Aug. 1873–Sept. 1873

Capt. Loomis L. Langdon
1st U.S. Artillery, Co. M / Sept. 1873–Dec. 1873

NOTES

Introduction

1. John R. Weaver II, *A Legacy in Brick and Stone: American Coastal Defense Forts of the Third System*, xiv–xv.

2. Ibid., 3–4; Lewis, *Seacoast Fortifications of the United States*, 37–38.

3. Weaver, *Legacy in Brick and Stone*, 6–9; Lewis, *Seacoast Fortifications*, 4.

4. Weaver, 10–11; Cullum, *Biographical Register of the Officers and Graduates of the U.S. Military Academy at West Point, New York*, 2: 371–73.

5. Smith, "The Corps of Engineers and National Defense in Antebellum America, 1815–1860."

6. Edward L. Widmer, *Young America: The Flowering of Democracy in New York City*, 36–39.

7. Robert D. Sampson, *John L. O'Sullivan and His Times*, 194–95.

8. Sutherland, "Fort Jefferson and American Nationalism: A Research Note."

9. Weaver, *Legacy in Brick and Stone*, 12–13.

10. Sampson, *John L. O'Sullivan*, 196–97.

11. Peskin, *Winfield Scott and the Profession of Arms*, 194–205, 216–24.

12. Weigley, *The American Way of War: A History of United States Military Strategy and Policy*, 59–76; Skelton, *American Profession of Arms*, 292–93.

13. Skelton, *American Profession of Arms*, 293.

14. Moten, *The Delafield Commission and the American Military Profession*, 194.

15. Skelton, *American Profession of Arms*, 140–41.

16. Ibid., 140–41, 293.

Chapter 1. Defender of a Young America: 1824–1859

1. U.S. Congress, Senate, *Documents Relating to the Bill Authorizing an Examination and Survey of the Harbor of Charleston and the Coast of Florida*.

2. Quoted in J. B. Holder, "The Dry Tortugas."

3. U.S. Congress, House of Representatives, *Report of the House Committee on Military Affairs*, 28th Congress, 1st Session, 2: 1–19.

4. Bearss, *Historic Structure Report: Fort Jefferson 1846–1898*, 7 (hereafter cited as *Fort Jefferson*).

5. Davis, "History of Juan Ponce de Leon's Voyage to Florida," 21.

6. Calvin Shedd to Dear Wife, June 9, 1862, Collection of the Civil War Letters of Calvin Shedd, University of Miami Library, Florida (hereafter cited as Shedd Collection).

7. Davis, "History of Juan Ponce de Leon," 40–41. The quotation is from a translation of Antonio de Herrera's *Historia General*, 1601.

8. William Pinckney to Pleasonton, April 27, 1826, U.S. Treasury Department, Letters Received, Records Group 26, National Archives and Records Administration, Washington, D.C. (hereafter cited as RG 26, National Archives).

9. Capt. Barnard to Engineer Department, November 14, 1844, U.S. Army, Chief of Engineers, Letters Received, Records Group 77, National Archives, Washington, D.C. (hereafter cited as RG 77, National Archives).

10. William Pinckney to Pleasonton, October 1, 1826, Letters Received, RG 26, National Archives.

11. Executive Order, September 17, 1845.

12. "Report of the Secretary of War, to the President, for 1845, and Accompanying Documents," *United States Democratic Review*, 291–92.

13. Hurley, *Lighthouses of the Dry Tortugas*, 22.

14. J. B. Holder, "The Dry Tortugas," 260.

15. Warner, *Generals in Blue: Lives of the Union Commanders*, 575–76.

16. Totten to Fraser, July 27, 1846, Chief of Engineers, Letters Sent, RG 77, National Archives.

17. Bearss, *Fort Jefferson*, 33.

18. Architectural Drawing by Lt. M. C. Meigs, December 1845, RG 77, National Archives.

19. "Daily Time Books and Paybooks of Civilian Laborers," Records Group 393, vol. 5, installation 221, item 23, November–December 1846, National Archives and Records Administration, Washington, D.C. (hereafter cited as RG 393, National Archives).

20. Wright to Totten, November 29, 1846, and January 7, 1847, Chief of Engineers, Letters Received, RG 77, National Archives.

21. Monthly Report of Construction, December 1846, and Annual Report of Construction, 1847, RG 393, vol. 5, installation 221, items 18, 19, National Archives; Vinson, Gibraltar of the Gulf: A Constructional History of Fort Jefferson, Dry Tortugas, 1844–1875, 48–49.

22. Manucy, "The Gibraltar of the Gulf of Mexico," 308.

23. Whitehurst to Wright, July 12, 1847, Chief of Engineers, Letters Received, RG 77, National Archives; Hurley, *Lighthouses of the Dry Tortugas*, 20.

24. Wright to Totten, July 21, 1847, Chief of Engineers, Letters Received, RG 77, National Archives.

25. War Department, Adjutant General Office, General Order no. 38, November 4, 1850.

26. "Our Sea-Coast Defense and Fortification System," *Putnam's Monthly Magazine*, 323.

27. Vinson, Gibraltar of the Gulf, appendix 2, iii.

28. Totten to Superintending Engineers, March 22, 1855, Chief of Engineers, Letters Sent, RG 77, National Archives; Vinson, Gibraltar of the Gulf, 54.

29. Totten to Wright, April 9, 1855, Chief of Engineers, Letters Sent, RG 77, National Archives; "Annual Reports of Operations 1851–1860," in Bethel, *Slumbering Giant*, 20; Vinson, Gibraltar of the Gulf, 54–55.

30. "Our Sea-Coast Defense and Fortification System," 326.

31. Hurley, *Lighthouses of the Dry Tortugas*, 31; *Dictionary of American Biography*, s.v. Joseph G. Totten; Chief Engineer Totten was a member of the Lighthouse Board, 1851–58.

32. Cullum, *Biographical Register*, 1: 496–97.

33. Hurley, *Lighthouses of the Dry Tortugas*, 32–33.

34. Woodbury to Totten, August 30, 1856, Chief of Engineers, Letters Received, RG 77, National Archives.

35. Woodbury to Totten, May 19, 1857 and October 5, 1857, Chief of Engineers, Letters Received, RG 77, National Archives; Vinson, Gibraltar of the Gulf, 67.

36. Ellsworth, "Raiford and Abercrombie: Pensacola's Premier Antebellum Manufacturer," 251–55.

37. "Crary's Improved Brick-Making Machine," *Scientific American*, 1–2.

38. Bearss, *Fort Jefferson*, 174–75.

39. Morton, *Letter to the Hon. John B. Floyd, Secretary of War*.

40. Moten, *The Delafield Commission*, 175, 193.

41. Morton, *Letter to the Hon. John B. Floyd*.

42. Morton, *Memoir on American Fortification Submitted to the Hon. John B. Floyd, Secretary of War*, 1859, 3–7.

43. "The Army Report of Secretary Floyd," *United States Democratic Review*, 130.

44. *Dictionary of American Biography*, s.v.v. Joseph Bassett Holder and Joseph Gilbert Totten.

45. Emily Holder, "At the Dry Tortugas during the War: A Lady's Journal," *Californian Illustrated Magazine*, (Jan. 1892), 87–93.

46. Ibid., Feb. 1892, 179–89; Eighth Census of the United States, 1860, Schedule 1 (Population), Garden Key (Tortugas), Monroe County, Florida, 64.

47. Bearss, *Fort Jefferson*, 177–78.

Chapter 2. A Union Threatened and the Outbreak of War: 1860–1861

1. DeRussy to Woodbury, March 18, 1859, Superintending Engineer, Letters Received, RG 393, vol. 5, installation 221, National Archives.

2. Annual Reports of Construction, 1860, Fort Jefferson Engineer Files, RG 393, National Archives.

3. Bearss, *Fort Jefferson*, 178.

4. Vinson, Gibraltar of the Gulf, 78–79.

5. Eighth Census of the United States, Schedule 1 (Free Inhabitants), Garden Key (Tortugas), Monroe County, Florida, 64.

6. E. Holder, "Dry Tortugas during the War," *Californian*, (Jan. 1892), 93, and (Feb. 1892), 179.

7. Weigley, *Quartermaster General*, 66–68, 108–12; Warner, *Generals in Blue*, 318–19.

8. Meigs to DeRussy, October 6, 1860, Chief of Engineers, Letters Received, and DeRussy to Meigs and Woodbury, October 11, 1860, Letters Sent, both in RG 77, National Archives.

9. Ellsworth, "Raiford and Abercrombie," 247–60.

10. U.S. War Department, *War of the Rebellion: A Compilation of the Official Records of the Union and Confederate Armies*, 128 vols., series I, vol. 52, pt. 1, 3–5 (hereafter cited as *O.R.*, with series, volume, part, and/or page numbers).

11. *O.R.*, series I, vol. 52, pt. 1, 4.

12. Meigs to Craven, November 15, 1860, Chief of Engineers, Letters Received, RG 77, National Archives; Weigley, *Quartermaster General*, 122–23; U.S. Naval War Records Office, *Official Records of the Union and Confederate Navies in the War of Rebellion*, 30 vols., series I, vol. 4, 3–4 (hereafter noted as *O.R.N.*, with series, volume, and page numbers).

13. *O.R.*, series I, vol. 1, 112.

14. Weigley, *Quartermaster General*, 126.

15. *O.R.*, series I, vol. 1, 345.

16. Ibid.

17. Toucey to Lieutenant Maffitt, January 5, 1861, *O.R.N.*, series I, vol. 4, 7.

18. Meigs' Letter Book, 1860, Library of Congress, 388–89, cited in Weigley, *Quartermaster General*, 120–21.

19. Welles, "Fort Pickens," 93–94.

20. Meigs to Lt. Col. R. E. DeRussy, January 15, 1861, *O.R.*, series I, vol. 52, pt. 1, 5–6.

21. E. Holder, "Dry Tortugas during the War," *Californian* (Feb. 1892), 185.

22. Ibid.

23. Arnold to Colonel Cooper, Adjutant General, January 18, 1861, *O.R.*, series I, vol. 1, 346.

24. "Fort Jefferson," *Harper's Weekly*, (February 23, 1861), 122.

25. Meigs to Totten, January 19, 1861, *O.R.*, series I, vol. 52, pt. 1, 1–3.

26. "Fort Jefferson," *Harper's Weekly*, (February 23, 1861), 122.

27. Arnold to Headquarters, U.S. Army, New York, January 23, 1861, *O.R.*, series I, vol. 1, 346–47.

28. Meigs to Totten, January 20, 1861, Chief of Engineers, Letters Received, RG 77, National Archives.

29. Lieutenant Craven to Secretary Toucey, January 23, 1861, *O.R.N.*, series I, vol. 4, 69.

30. Meigs to Totten, January 23, 1861, Chief of Engineers, Letters Received, RG 77, National Archives.

31. Meigs to Totten, January 25, 1861, *O.R.*, series I, vol. 52, pt. 1, 125–26.

32. Ibid.

33. Monthly Return, January 1861, Fort Jefferson, Records Group 94, Adjutant General's Office, microcopy M-617, roll 542, January 1861–December 1868, National Archives and Records Administration (hereafter cited as Monthly Return).

34. *O.R.*, series I, vol. 1, 345.

35. Meigs to Totten, January 26, 1861, Chief of Engineers, Letters Received, RG 77, National Archives.

36. Meigs to Totten, February 2, 1861, Chief of Engineers, Letters Received, RG 77, National Archives.

37. Vinson, Gibraltar of the Gulf, 88.

38. Totten to Meigs, February 11, 1861, Chief of Engineers, Letters Sent, RG 77, National Archives.

39. *O.R.*, series I, vol. 1, 587.

40. Ibid., 587–88. The fifth company, Battery M, Second Artillery, formerly stationed at Fort Brown, was to continue with the ship to New York.

41. Oates, *Rip Ford's Texas*, 318–19.

42. Thomas T. Smith, *The Old Army in Texas*, 103.

43. Major Porter to Assistant Adjutant General, March 23, 1861, *O.R.*, series I, vol. 52, pt. 1, 126.

44. Weigley, *Quartermaster General*, 128–29.

45. Morton to Totten, March 25, 1861, Chief of Engineers, Letters Received, RG 77, National Archives.

46. Morton to Totten, April 3, 1861, Chief of Engineers, Letters Received, and Totten to Morton, April 12 and May 2, 1861, Chief of Engineers, Letters Sent, both in RG 77, National Archives.

47. Monthly Return, March 1861.

48. Shinn, *Fort Jefferson and Its Commander 1861–2*, 20.

49. *O.R.*, series I, vol. 1, 365–66; *O.R.*, series I, vol. 52, pt. 1, 180.

50. Weigley, *Quartermaster General*, 145.

51. Col. Brown to the Secretary of the General-in-Chief, April 15, 1861, *O.R.*, series I, vol. 1, 376–77.

52. Ibid., 377.

53. *O.R.*, series I, vol. 1, 389–90.

54. Weigley, *Quartermaster General*, 150.

55. Brown to Arnold, April 22, 1861, *O.R.*, series I, vol. 1, 392–93.

56. *O.R.N.*, series I, vol. 4, 156–57, 163, 340.

57. E. Holder, "Dry Tortugas during the War," *Californian*, (March 1892), 274.

There is no later mention of the cannon; it may have been sold as salvage by the army.

58. Monthly Return, April 1861.

59. Totten to Army Headquarters, June 18, 1861, *O.R.*, series I, vol. 52, pt. 1, 179–80.

60. Shinn, *Fort Jefferson and Its Commander*, 17 (Robinson quotation); Schmidt, *A Civil War History of the 47th Regiment of Pennsylvania Veteran Volunteers*, 307 (hereafter cited as *47th Regiment*).

61. Shinn, *Fort Jefferson and Its Commander*, 21.

62. E. Holder, "Dry Tortugas during the War," *Californian*, (March 1892), 276–77.

63. Schmidt, *47th Regiment*, 66.

64. Monthly Return, July 1861.

65. "Attack on Camp of Wilson's Zouaves, on Santa Rosa Island," *Harper's Weekly*, (November 9, 1861), 705.

66. Abstract from the Returns for the Department of Florida, October, 1861, *O.R.*, series I, vol. 6, 672.

67. Manucy, "The Gibraltar of the Gulf of Mexico," 316.

68. Monthly Return, September 1861.

69. War Department, A.G.O., General Order no. 76, February 26, 1864.

70. Monthly Return, September 1861.

71. E. Holder, "Dry Tortugas during the War," *Californian*, (March 1892), 281–82.

72. Monthly Return, November 1861; E. Holder, "Dry Tortugas during the War," *Californian*, (March 1892), 278.

73. Thomas to Brown, December 20, 1861, *O.R.*, series I, vol. 6, 673.

74. Brown to Thomas, December 27, 1861, *O.R.*, series I, vol. 6, 673–74.

75. Monthly Return, December 1861.

76. Totten to Morton, June 18, 1861, Chief of Engineers, Letters Sent, RG 77, National Archives.

77. Sanger, *Statutes at Large . . . December 5, 1859 to March 3, 1863*, 12:261–64.

Chapter 3. Bad Rations and Boredom in Paradise: 1862

1. "Stations of Vessels Composing the Gulf Blockading Squadron," January 23, 1862, *O.R.N.*, series I, vol. 17, 71.

2. War Department, A.G.O., General Order no. 3, January 11, 1862, in *O.R.*, series I, vol. 6, 217–18.

3. Warner, *Generals in Blue*, 42–43.

4. Monthly Returns, January and February, 1862.

5. Sergeant Calvin Shedd to wife Augusta and children, March 2, 1862, Shedd Collection.

6. E. Holder, "Dry Tortugas during the War," *Californian*, (April 1892), 397–403.

7. Little, *The Seventh Regiment New Hampshire Volunteers in the War of the Rebellion*, 36–39; Calvin Shedd to family, March 15, 1862, Shedd Collection.

8. Little, *Seventh Regiment*, 460–63.

9. Calvin Shedd to Dear Ones at home, March 6, 1862, Shedd Collection.

10. Little, *Seventh Regiment*, 28–34; Calvin Shedd to family, March 15, 1862, Shedd Collection.

11. E. Holder, "Dry Tortugas during the War," *Californian*, (April 1892), 397–98.

12. Calvin Shedd to Dear Wife & Children, April 19, 1862, Shedd Collection.

13. Phillips to McFarland, May 28, 1862, cited in Manucy, "The Gibraltar of the Gulf of Mexico," 316.

14. *O.R.,* series II, vol. 1, 814.

15. Ibid.

16. Calvin Shedd to Dear Wife, March 6, 1862 and April 25, 1862, Shedd Collection.

17. Weaver, *Legacy in Brick and Stone*, 145–47; *O.R.N.*, series I, vol. 12, 731–32.

18. Weaver, *Legacy in Brick and Stone*, 145–47.

19. Weaver, *Legacy in Brick and Stone*, 60–61.

20. Calvin Shedd to Dear Wife & Children, April 2, 1862, Shedd Collection; *O.R.*, series I, vol. 14, 410.

21. Calvin Shedd to Dear Wife & Children, March 15, 1862, Shedd Collection; Monthly Return, March 1862.

22. Shedd, March 24 and 26, 1862, April 2, 1862, Shedd Collection.

23. Calvin Shedd to Dear Wife and Children, April 2 and 19, 1862, Shedd Collection.

24. Calvin Shedd to My Dear Wife and Children, May 13, 1862, Shedd Collection.

25. Monthly Returns, April and May, 1862.

26. Special Order no. 12, District of Key West and Tortugas, March 5, 1862; Morton to Totten, March 5, 1862, Chief of Engineers, Letters Received, RG 77, National Archives.

27. Morton to Totten, May 25, 1862, Chief of Engineers, Letters Received, RG 77, National Archives.

28. Schmidt, *The Civil War in Florida: A Military History*, 3: xxxv.

29. Vinson, Gibraltar of the Gulf, 98–99.

30. Monthly Return, June 1862.

31. E. Holder, "Dry Tortugas during the War," *Californian*, (April 1892), 400–1; Dyer, *A Compendium of the War of the Rebellion . . . [New York State].*

32. *O.R.*, series I, vol. 14, 367.

33. McFarland to Totten, September 11, 1862, Chief of Engineers, Letters Received, RG 77, National Archives.

34. Monthly Returns, July and August, 1862.

35. Schmidt, *47th Regiment*, 303; Vinson, Gibraltar of the Gulf, 96.

36. Dr. C. H. Crane to Major W. P. Prentice, A.A.G., Dept. of the South, *O.R.*, series I, vol. 14, 384.

37. Monthly Returns, August–December 1862.

38. Ibid.

39. Brig. Gen. John Milton Brannen to Col. Tilghman H. Good, December 16, 1862, in Schmidt, *47th Regiment*, 291.

40. Ibid., 293, 303.

41. E. Holder, "Dry Tortugas during the War," *Californian*, (April 1892), 400.

42. A. O'D., "Thirty Months at the Dry Tortugas," *Galaxy Miscellany*, (February 1869), 282–83.

43. Bethel, *Slumbering Giant*, 55; Vinson, *Gibraltar of the Gulf*, 97.

44. Schmidt, *47th Regiment*, 306.

Chapter 4. Construction, Convicts, and the Pennsylvania Volunteers: 1863

1. *O.R.*, series I, vol. 14, 410. General Hunter's estimate of the Fort Jefferson garrison was very low and probably based on outdated reports; actual strength was 377 as of the January 1863 monthly return.

2. Diary of Cpl. G. W. Albert, January 20, 1863, in Schmidt, *47th Regiment*, 314.

3. E. Holder, "Dry Tortugas during the War," *Californian*, (Feb. 1892), 180.

4. Totten to McFarland, June 19, 1863, Chief of Engineers, Letters Sent, RG 77, National Archives.

5. E. Holder, "Dry Tortugas during the War," *Californian*, (June 1892), 102–9.

6. Schmidt, *47th Regiment*, 322–23.

7. Monthly Return, March 1863.

8. *O.R.*, series I, vol. 27, 712–13.

9. Bearss, *Fort Jefferson*, 234–35.

10. J. B. Holder, "Along the Florida Reef," pt. 4, *Harper's*, (April 1871), 821–22.

11. Ibid.

12. Schmidt, *47th Regiment*, 329–30.

13. Ibid., 326, 328.

14. Ibid., 330.

15. Monthly Return, April 1863.

16. Schmidt, *47th Regiment*, 335–36.

17. Ibid., 339.

18. Sergeant Calvin Shedd to My Dear Family, May 4, 1862, Shedd Collection.

19. Schmidt, *47th Regiment*, 339, 344, 346, 349.

20. Monthly Return, June 1863.

21. "Stations of Vessels of the East Gulf Blockading Squadron," July 15, 1863, *O.R.N.*, series I, vol. 17, 502; E. Holder, "Dry Tortugas during the War," *Californian*, (April 1892), 400.

22. Edward Van Sice to Hon. Gideon Welles, June 13, 1863, *O.R.N.*, series I, vol.

17, 467; Lt. Cmdr. W. H. Dana to Hon. Gideon Welles, October 8, 1863, *O.R.N.,* series I, vol. 20, 615.

23. J. B. Holder, "Along the Florida Reef," pt. 4, 828.

24. Monthly Returns, April, June, and November 1863.

25. E. Holder, "Dry Tortugas during the War," *Californian,* (June 1892), 102–9.

Chapter 5. War's End and the Arrival of the Conspirators: 1864–1865

1. Report of Major General F. J. Herron, President of Commission, December 13, 1863, *O.R.,* series I, vol. 26, pt. 1, 475–76.

2. Ibid., 475.

3. General Orders no. 90, Department of the Gulf, December 30, 1863, *O.R.,* series I, vol. 26, pt. 1, 476–79; Monthly Return, January 1864.

4. E. Holder, "Dry Tortugas during the War," *Californian,* (June 1892), 102–9.

5. Schmidt, *47th Regiment,* 429; Special Orders no. 39, Department of the Gulf, New Orleans, February 13, 1864, *O.R.,* series I, vol. 34, pt. 2, 316.

6. Monthly Return, March 1864.

7. Diary of Sergeant Harrison Herrick, March 27–30, 1864, in Bethel, *Slumbering Giant,* 32.

8. Ibid., April 25–26, 1864, 32; Monthly Return, April 1864.

9. Diary of Sergeant Herrick, May 1864, in Bethel, *Slumbering Giant,* 32; Monthly Return, May 1864.

10. Welles to Farragut, May 9, May 19, and September 14, 1864, all in *O.R.N.,* ser. I, vol. 21, 268–69, 288, 642.

11. Diary of Sergeant Herrick, June 1, 1864, 32; Monthly Return, June–September 1864.

12. Meketa, "A Poetic Plea from Prison," 28–32.

13. Monthly Returns, November–December 1864.

14. Diary of Sergeant Herrick, November 10–13, 1864, in Bethel, *Slumbering Giant,* 33; Henry B. Whitney Diary, November 13, 1864, Perkins Library, Duke University, Durham, N.C.

15. E. Holder, "Dry Tortugas during the War," *Californian,* (August 1892), 388–95; Henry B. Whitney Diary, November 10–14, 1864.

16. E. Holder, "Dry Tortugas during the War," *Californian,* (August 1892), 390–91.

17. J. B. Holder, "The Dry Tortugas," 260.

18. Ibid., 264; Diary of Sergeant Herrick, March 19, 1865, in Bethel, *Slumbering Giant,* 33.

19. Diary of Sergeant Herrick, April 20, 1865, in Bethel, *Slumbering Giant,* 33.

20. E. Holder, "Dry Tortugas during the War," *Californian* (Aug. 1892), 392.

21. Henry B. Whitney Diary, April 22, 1865.

22. Ibid., March 10, 1864.

23. Bearss, *Fort Jefferson*, 258–59.

24. Henry B. Whitney Diary, July 24, 1865.

25. Ibid.

26. Kauffman, *Samuel Bland Arnold: Memoirs of a Lincoln Conspirator*, 65 (hereafter cited as *Memoirs*).

27. E. Holder, "Dry Tortugas during the War," (Aug. 1892), 391–92.

28. Mudd, *Life of Samuel Mudd*, 124–25; Monthly Return, June 1866; Wythe had been assigned on June 8, 1866.

29. E. Holder, "Dry Tortugas during the War," (Sept. 1892), 561–62. Although Samuel Arnold evidently appeared to be younger, Dr. Samuel Mudd was actually three years his junior.

30. Kauffman, *Memoirs*, 75.

31. Robert M. Utley, *Cavalier in Buckskin*, 36–37.

32. Henry B. Whitney Diary, August 1 and 16, 1865; Monthly Return, August 1865.

33. A. O'D., "Thirty Months in the Dry Tortugas," 286–87.

34. E. Holder, "Dry Tortugas during the War," (Sept. 1892), 561.

35. Mudd, *Life of Samuel Mudd*, 118.

36. Brig. Gen. John Newton to A.A.G., Washington D.C., October 1865, RG 94, microcopy M-619, roll 391, file no. 507 N 1865, National Archives.

37. Starr, *Colonel Grenfell's Wars*, 278–79.

38. Bearss, *Fort Jefferson*, 288–89.

39. Major Wentworth to A.A.G., Dept. of Florida, October 24, 1865, RG 94, microcopy M-619, roll 391, National Archives.

40. Bearss, *Fort Jefferson*, 289; McFarland to War Department, September 25, 1866, Chief of Engineers, Letters Received, RG 77, National Archives, cited in Vinson, Gibraltar of the Gulf, 104.

41. Special Order, Headquarters, District of Middle Florida, October 20, 1865, RG 94, microcopy M-619, roll 391, National Archives.

42. A.A.G. to Major General Sheridan, October–December 1865, RG 94, microcopy M-619, roll 391, file no. 507 N 1865, National Archives.

43. Ibid.

44. E. Holder, "Dry Tortugas during the War, (Aug. 1892), 390–91.

45. Mudd, *Life of Samuel Mudd*, 139.

46. Kauffman, *Memoirs*, 77.

47. Monthly Return, December 1865.

48. Mudd, *Life of Samuel Mudd*, 148–50.

49. Ibid.

Chapter 6. The Nation's Most Notorious Prison: 1866–1868

1. A. O'D., "Thirty Months at the Dry Tortugas," *Galaxy Miscellany*, 282.

2. Kauffman, *Memoirs*, 64.

3. Mudd, *Life of Samuel Mudd*, 154–55.

4. Ibid., 161.

5. Monthly Return, April 1866; the section on correspondence notes that a letter was received from the War Department April 19, 1866, stating that Dr. Holder would return to Fort Jefferson for the summer. The monthly return for October 1866 recorded that the contract ended on October 31, 1866.

6. Kauffman, *Memoirs*, 67; Mudd, *Life of Samuel Mudd*, 161.

7. Mudd, *Life of Samuel Mudd*, 162–63.

8. Ibid., 165.

9. Kauffman, *Memoirs*, 81.

10. Mudd, *Life of Samuel Mudd*, 173, 175.

11. Henry B. Whitney Diary, March 28, 1864.

12. Kauffman, *Memoirs*, 87.

13. Ibid., 78.

14. Ibid., 83, 85–86.

15. Mudd, *Life of Samuel Mudd*, 185; Monthly Return, August 1866.

16. Monthly Return, January 1867; Mudd, *Life of Samuel Mudd*, 220.

17. Cited in Starr, *Colonel Grenfell's Wars*, 284.

18. Kauffman, *Memoirs*, 88.

19. Ibid., 89.

20. Kauffman, *Memoirs*, 89–92.

21. Bradley T. Johnson to Col. George Grenfell, October 9, 1866, RG 94, microcopy M-619, roll 451, National Archives.

22. New York *World*, November 1, 1866, 5.

23. Ibid.

24. Ibid.

25. Kauffman, *Memoirs*, 93–94.

26. Report of Brevet Lieutenant Colonel George L. Gillespie to Adjutant General, November 25, 1866, RG 94, microcopy M-619, roll 451, National Archives.

27. Kauffman, *Memoirs*, 95.

28. Adjutant General to Bvt. Brig. Gen. Bennett H. Hill, December 24, 1866, RG 94, microcopy M-619, roll 451, National Archives.

29. Sworn Statement, Brevet Major Benjamin Rittenhouse to Brevet Lieutenant Colonel George L. Gillespie, November 25, 1866, RG 94, microcopy M-619, roll 451, National Archives.

30. Adjutant General to Major General Philip H. Sheridan, March 29, 1867, RG 94, microcopy M-619, roll 451, National Archives.

31. Kauffman, *Memoirs*, 105–6.

32. Richter, *The Army in Texas during Reconstruction: 1865–1870*, 28–30.

33. Mudd, *Life of Samuel Mudd*, 252; Kauffman, *Memoirs*, 108–9; Monthly Return, August 1867, notes that Winters died August 1, 1867.

34. Kauffman, *Memoirs*, 169n; Mudd, *Life of Samuel Mudd*, 255–56.

35. E. Holder, "Dry Tortugas during the War," (May 1892), 585–88.

36. Mudd, *Life of Samuel Mudd*, 125; E. Holder, "Dry Tortugas during the War," (May 1892), 586–87; Kauffman, *Memoirs*, 72.

37. Kauffman, *Memoirs*, 110–11; Monthly Returns, August–October 1867; Arnold states thirty-seven deaths, but of these eight were civilians or prisoners.

38. Mudd, *Life of Samuel Mudd*, 258–9; Kauffman, *Memoirs*, 111.

39. Monthly Return, September 1867.

40. Mudd, *Life of Samuel Mudd*, 267, 271.

41. Ibid., 270–71.

42. Ibid., 280; Kauffman, *Memoirs*, 113.

43. J. B. Holder, "The Dry Tortugas," 261.

44. Cullum, *Biographical Register*, 1: 405–6.

45. Bearss, *Fort Jefferson*, 296.

46. Kauffman, *Memoirs*, 117.

47. Starr, *Colonel Grenfell's Wars*, 320–22.

48. Ibid., 324–25.

49. A. O'D., "Thirty Months in the Dry Tortugas," 287.

50. Starr, *Colonel Grenfell's Wars*, 327.

51. Ibid., 332.

52. Ibid., 322–23; Mudd, *Life of Samuel Mudd*, 305.

53. Monthly Return, May 1868.

54. Rogers, "The Eutaw Prisoners: Federal Confrontation with Violence in Reconstruction Alabama," 101–2.

55. Ibid.

56. Ibid., 104–5.

57. Ibid., 109.

58. Kauffman, *Memoirs*, 120.

59. Mudd, *Life of Samuel Mudd*, 308.

60. Rogers, "The Eutaw Prisoners," 116–17.

61. Mudd, *Life of Samuel Mudd*, 309–10.

62. Ibid.

63. Ibid., 315.

Chapter 7. The Fortress Abandoned: 1869–1874

1. A. O'D., "Thirty Months at the Dry Tortugas," *Galaxy*, 288.

2. "Editor's Historical Record," *Harper's*, 40.

3. Cullum, *Biographical Register*, 2: 255.

4. Monthly Return, February 1869—these were batteries F, I, L, and M of the 3rd U.S. Artillery; Bearss, *Fort Jefferson*, 304–5.

5. Bush, *A Short History of the 5th Regiment U.S. Artillery*, 44.

6. Bearss, *Fort Jefferson*, 303.

7. Fort Jefferson, Monthly Report, May 1873, Chief of Engineers, Letters Received, RG 77, National Archives.

8. Bearss, *Fort Jefferson*, 336.

9. Bethel, *Slumbering Giant*, 51.

10. Ibid., 50; Bearss, *Fort Jefferson*, 336–37; Shinn, *Fort Jefferson and Its Commander*, 19.

11. Captain Langdon to Adjutant General, Department of the South, September 20, 1873, Chief of Engineers, Letters Received, RG 77, National Archives.

12. Bearss, *Fort Jefferson*, 333.

13. Bradford, *The Virginius Affair*.

14. Monthly Returns, November 1873 and January 1874; Bearss, *Fort Jefferson*, 338.

15. "Editor's Historical Record," *Harper's*, 40.

16. Vinson, Gibraltar of the Gulf, 108.

BIBLIOGRAPHY

Primary Sources

Arnold, Samuel Bland. *Defense and Prison Experiences of a Lincoln Conspirator.* Hattiesburg, Miss.: Book Farm, 1943.

"Attack on Camp of Wilson's Zouaves, on Santa Rosa Island." *Harper's Weekly* 5, no. 254 (November 9, 1861): 705.

Bush, James Clark. *A Short History of the 5th Regiment U.S. Artillery.* Governor's Island, N.Y. [*s.n.*], 1895.

Clark, Lewis H. *Military History of Wayne County, N.Y.: Military Register. Wayne County in the Civil War, 1861–1865.* Sodus, N.Y.: Clark, Hulett and Gaylord, 1883.

"Crary's Improved Brick-Making Machine." *Scientific American* 4 (January 5, 1861): 1–2.

Cullum, George Washington. *Biographical Register of Officers and Graduates of the U.S. Military Academy at West Point, New York.* 2 Vols. New York: D. Van Nostrund, 1868.

"Dr. Mudd's Attempt to Escape from Dry Tortugas." *Harper's Weekly* 9, no. 460 (October 21, 1865): 1.

Dyer, Frederick H. *A Compendium of the War of the Rebellion Compiled and Arranged from Official Records of the Federal and Confederate Armies [New York State].* Des Moines, Iowa: Dyer Publishing Company, 1908.

"Editor's Historical Record." *Harper's New Monthly Magazine* 49, no. 292 (November 1874): 40.

"Fort Jefferson." *Harper's Weekly* 5, no. 217 (February 23, 1861): 121–22.

Holder, Emily. "At the Dry Tortugas During the War: A Lady's Journal." *Californian Illustrated Magazine,* vol. 1, no. 2 (January 1892)–vol. 2, no. 4 (September 1892).

Holder, Dr. Joseph B. "Along the Florida Reef." *Harper's New Monthly Magazine* 42–43 (June 1868–April 1871).

———. "The Atlantic Right Whales." *Bulletin of the American Museum of Natural History* 5, no. 217 (May 1883): 121–22.

———. "The Dry Tortugas." *Harper's Monthly Magazine* 37 (July 1868): 260–7.

———. *History of the American Fauna.* New York: Virtue and Yorston for the American Museum of Natural History, 1877.

Holder, Joseph B., and Rev. J. G. Wood. *Animate Creation: Popular Edition of "Our Living World," a Natural History.* New York: S. Hess, 1898.

Kauffman, Michael W., ed. *Samuel Bland Arnold: Memoirs of a Lincoln Conspirator.* Bowie, Md.: Heritage Books, 1995.

Morton, Lieutenant James St. C. *Letter to the Hon. John B. Floyd, Secretary of War Presenting for His Consideration a New Plan for the Fortification of Certain Points of the Seacoast of the United States.* Washington, D.C.: W. A. Harris, 1858.

———. *Memoir on American Fortification Submitted to the Hon. John B. Floyd, Secretary of War.* Washington, D.C.: W. A. Harris, 1859.

Mudd, Nettie. *The Life of Dr. Samuel A. Mudd.* New York: Neale Publishing Company, 1906; reprint, Roger D. Mudd, 1962.

Oates, Stephen B., ed. *Rip Ford's Texas.* Austin: University of Texas Press, 1963.

O'D., A. "Thirty Months at the Dry Tortugas." *Galaxy Miscellany* 7 (February 1869): 282–88.

"Our Sea-Coast Defense and Fortification System." *Putnam's Monthly Magazine of American Literature, Science and Art* 7 (March 1856): 314–26.

"Report of the Secretary of War, to the President, for 1845, and Accompanying Documents." *United States Democratic Review* 18 (April 1846): 291–92.

Sanger, George P., ed. *The Statutes at Large, Treaties, and Proclamations of the United States of America from December 5, 1859 to March 3, 1863.* Vol. 12. Boston, Mass.: 1863.

Shedd, Calvin. Collection of the Civil War Letters of Calvin Shedd, University of Miami Library, Florida.

Shinn, Josiah H. *Fort Jefferson and Its Commander 1861–2.* Governor's Island, N.Y.: privately printed, 1910.

"The Army Report of Secretary Floyd." *United States Democratic Review* 41 (February 1858): 130.

U.S. Army, Adjutant General. Adjutant General Reservation File 1800–1886. Records Group 94, Textual Records of the Army Office of the Adjutant General, National Archives, Washington, D.C.

U.S. Army, Chief of Engineers. Letters Sent: 1812–1869, and Letters Received: 1826–1866. Records Group 77, Textual Records of the Office of the Army Chief of Engineers, National Archives, Washington, D.C.

U.S. Army, Continental Army Commands. Installation 221, Fort Jefferson, Dry Tortugas, Florida. Records Group 393, Records of the Continental Army Commands, vol. 5, National Archives, Washington, D.C.

U.S. Congress, House of Representatives. *Report of the House Committee on Military Affairs,* 28th Congress, 1st Session, 1834, report 407, vol. 2.

U.S. Congress, Senate. *Documents Relating to the Bill Authorizing an Examination and Survey of the Harbor of Charleston and the Coast of Florida*, 18th Congress, 1st Session, 1824, Senate document 76.

U.S. Naval War Records Office. *Official Records of the Union and Confederate Navies in the War of Rebellion.* 30 vols. Washington, D.C.: Government Printing Office, 1894–1922.

U.S. Treasury Department. Records Group 26, Textual Records of the Department of the Treasury, National Archives and Records Administration, Washington, D.C.

U.S. War Department. *War of the Rebellion: A Compilation of the Official Records of the Union and Confederate Armies.* 128 vols. Washington, D.C.: Government Printing Office, 1880–1901.

Welles, Gideon. "Fort Pickens." *Galaxy Miscellany* 11 (January 1871): 92–108.

Whitney, Henry B. Diary, 1862–1865. Manuscript Department, Collection 5715. William R. Perkins Library, Duke University, Durham, N.C.

Wilder, John. "Out on the Reef." *Atlantic Monthly* 22 (August 1868): 176–89.

Secondary Sources

Bearss, Edwin C. *Historic Structure Report: Fort Jefferson: 1846–1898, Fort Jefferson National Monument, Florida.* Denver, Co.: U.S. Department of the Interior, National Park Service, Denver Service Center, 1983.

Bethel, Rodman. *A Slumbering Giant of the Past: Fort Jefferson.* Hialeah, Fla.: W. L. Litho., 1979.

Bradford, Richard H. *The Virginius Affair.* Boulder: Colorado Associated University Press, 1980.

Brown, William E., Jr., and Ruthanne D. Vogel, curators Calvin Shedd Papers. University of Miami, Otto G. Richter Library, Archives and Special Collections, http://www.library.miami.edu/archives/shedd/index.htm (accessed May 18, 2004).

Carter III, Samuel. *The Riddle of Dr. Mudd.* New York: G. P. Putnam's Sons, 1974.

Davis, T. Frederick. "History of Juan Ponce de Leon's Voyage to Florida: First Voyage and Discovery of Florida," *Florida Historical Quarterly* 14, no. 1 (July 1935), 15–34.

Ellsworth, Lucias F. "Raiford and Abercrombie: Pensacola's Premier Antebellum Manufacturer." *Florida Historical Quarterly* 52 (January 1974): 247–60.

England, George Allan. *Isles of Romance.* New York: Century Company, 1929.

Higdon, Hal. *The Union vs. Dr. Mudd.* Chicago: Follett Publishing Company, 1964.

Hurley, Neil E. *Lighthouses of the Dry Tortugas.* Aiea, Hi.: Historic Lighthouse Publishers, 1994.

Lewis, Emanuel Raymond. *Seacoast Fortifications of the United States: An Introductory History.* Washington, D.C.: Smithsonian Institution Press, 1979.

Little, Henry F. W. *The Seventh Regiment New Hampshire Volunteers in the War of the Rebellion.* Concord: Seventh New Hampshire Veteran Association, 1896.

Malone, Dumas, ed. *Dictionary of American Biography*, s.v. Holder, Joseph Bassett. New York: Charles Scribner's Sons, 1932, 7:140–41.

Making of America, Primary Sources accessible through the University of Michigan and Cornell University, http://cdl.library.cornell.edu/moa/, and http://hti.umich.edu/m/moagrp/ (accessed July 25, 2005).

Manucy, Albert. "The Gibraltar of the Gulf of Mexico." *Florida Historical Quarterly* 21 (1943): 303–31.

Meketa, Jacqueline Dorgan. "A Poetic Plea from Prison." *Civil War Times Illustrated* 30, no. 1 (1991): 28–32.

Meneely, A. Howard. *The War Department, 1861*. New York: Columbia University Press, 1928.

Moore, Jamie W. *The Fortifications Board 1816–1828, and the Definition of National Security*. Charleston, S.C.: Citadel Press, 1981.

Moten, Matthew. *The Delafield Commission and the American Military Profession*. College Station: Texas A & M Press, 2000.

National Park Service, Civil War Soldiers and Sailors System, http://www.itd.nps.gov/cwss/soldiers.htm (accessed June 3, 2004).

National Park Service, Dry Tortugas National Park. "City on the Sea: A Collection of Dry Tortugas Personal Histories" (CD-ROM). U.S. Department of the Interior, March 2004.

Peskin, Allan. *Winfield Scott and the Profession of Arms*. Kent, Ohio: Kent State University Press, 2003.

Richter, William L. *The Army in Texas during Reconstruction: 1865–1870*. College Station: Texas A&M University Press, 1987.

Robinson, Willard B. *American Forts: Architectural Form and Function*. Urbana: University of Illinois Press, 1977.

Rogers, William Warren, Jr. "The Eutaw Prisoners: Federal Confrontation with Violence in Reconstruction Alabama." *Alabama Review* 43 (April 1990): 98–121.

Sampson, Robert D. *John L. O'Sullivan and his Times*. Kent: Ohio State University Press, 2003.

Schmidt, Lewis G. *A Civil War History of the 47th Regiment of Pennsylvania Veteran Volunteers*. Allentown, Pa.: L. G. Schmidt, 1986.

———. *The Civil War in Florida: A Military History*. 3 vols. Allentown, Penn.: L. G. Schmidt, 1989.

Skelton, William B. *An American Profession of Arms*. Lawrence: University of Kansas Press, 1992.

Smith, Mark Andrew, "The Corps of Engineers and National Defense in Antebellum America, 1815–1860." Ph.D. diss., University of Alabama, 2004.

Smith, Thomas T. *The Old Army in Texas*. Austin: Texas State Historical Association, 2000.

Starr, Stephen Z. *Colonel Grenfell's Wars*. Baton Rouge: Louisiana State University Press, 1971.

Sutherland, Robert W., Jr. "Fort Jefferson and American Nationalism: A Research Note," Cornell College, http://people.cornellcollege.edu/rsutherland/ftjeffam-natrnmark027.doc (accessed September 18, 2004).

Utley, Robert M. *Cavalier in Buckskin: George Armstrong Custer and the Western Military Frontier*. Norman: University of Oklahoma Press, 1988.

Van Buren, Lin. "New York Civil War Soldiers Buried in Fort Jefferson Cemetery in Florida," http://www.rootsweb.com/~nyrensse/flcem3.htm (accessed August 5, 2004).

Vinson, Henry T., Jr., Gibraltar of the Gulf: A Constructional History of Fort Jefferson, Dry Tortugas, 1844–1875. Master's thesis, Florida State University, 1992.

Warner, Ezra J., *Generals in Blue: Lives of the Union Commanders*. Baton Rouge: Louisiana State University Press, 1964.

Weaver, John R. II. *A Legacy in Brick and Stone: American Coastal Defense Forts of the Third System, 1816–1867*. Missoula, Mont.: Pictorial Histories Publishing Company, 2001.

Weigley, Russell F. *Quartermaster General of the Union Army: A Biography of M. C. Meigs*. New York: Columbia University Press, 1959.

———. *The American Way of War: A History of United States Military Strategy and Policy*. New York: Macmillan, 1973.

Widmer, Edward L. *Young America: The Flowering of Democracy in New York City*. New York: Oxford University Press, 2000.

INDEX

INDEX

fect on, 69–70; escape of, 30; among Fort Jefferson population groups, 61; freed by Col. J. Morgan, 64–65; New Enganders' sympathy with, 57–58, 59; removal to Fort Pickens, 45–46; replaced by prisoner-laborers, 50, 76; *v.* white workers in building construction, 16–17, 23, 25, 29, 45–46, 58–59

Slemmer, Adam J., 35

Slidell, John, 13

Slott, Captain, 115

Smallpox, 55–56, 61, 79

Smith, Edmund K., 85

Smith, Edward B., 78

Smith, Fred, 64

Smith, Harry, 111

Smith, Jared A., 128, 131

Smith, Joseph Sim, 111

Smithsonian Institution, 25, 122

South Carolina, State of, 70

Spangler, Edman, 88, 93, 113, 119, 124

Sprague, Charles F., 117

S.R. Mallory, clipper, 56

Stanton, Edwin, 96, 119

State of Georgia, steamship, 49

Stearns, R. A., 94

Steele, James, 117, 118

Sterling, John W., 94

Stone, Valentine H., 112, 134

Storrow, Samuel A., 125

Strayhorn, Samuel, 118

Swift, J. G., 3

Tallahassee, Fla., 104

Taney, Roger B., 29

Tattnall, Josiah, 10

Taylor, Charles, 78

Taylor, Zachary, 13

Texas, State of, 5, 12

Thomas, Edward, 113, 116

Thomas A. Scott, steamship, 93, 96

Thompson, John, 13, 16, 17

Thompson's Island. *See* Key West

Tinelli, Louis W., 63–64, 70, 96, 133

Todd, John W., 50

Tonawanda, steamship, 92

Tonsberghus, bark, 126

Toombs, William, 55, 61, 64, 65

Tortugas, schooner, 26, 43, 95

Tortugas Harbor Light, 22

Totten, Joseph Gilbert, 1, 3, 6, 8, 17, 26, 47, 122

Toucey, Isaac, 34

Trans-Mississippi Confederacy, 85

Treaty of Guadalupe Hidalgo, 6

Twiggs, David E., 42

Tycoon, bark, 55

Union, Ala., 117

Union, steamship, 56

United States Capitol, 31

"United States Magazine and Democratic Review," 4

United States Military Academy, 3, 7, 8

United States Ships (U.S.S.): *Cayuga*, 75; *Chambers*, 54; *Crusader*, 34, 46; *Florida* (gunboat), 88; *Maine*, 129; *Mohawk*, 33, 35, 46; *Powhatan*, 46; *Rhode Island*, 52; *San Jacinto*, 74; *St. Louis*, 46; *Suffolk*, 77; *Thames*, 80; *Wyandotte*, 33, 46

United States War Department, 8

Vangeison, Virginius, 55

Van Linder, J., 83

Van Sice, Edward, 74–75

Vennard, Andrew B., 16

Vera Cruz, Mex., 6

Vermin, 61, 104

Verot, Bishop of Savannah, 101

Verplanck, Abraham, 135

Vicksburg, Miss., 67, 68

Victoria, Abraham, 78

Virginius, steamship, 128

Vogdes, Israel, 42

Thomas Reid (1947–2020) was lecturer in American history at Lamar University in Beaumont, Texas. He is the author of *Spartan Band: Burnett's 13th Texas Cavalry in the Civil War* and articles about the military history of the American Civil War.

Orange Journalism: Voices from Florida Newspapers, by Julian M. Pleasants (2003)

The Stranahans of Fort Lauderdale: A Pioneer Family of New River, by Harry A. Kersey Jr. (2003; first paperback edition, 2022)

Death in the Everglades: The Murder of Guy Bradley, America's First Martyr to Environmentalism, by Stuart B. McIver (2003; first paperback edition, 2009)

Jacksonville: The Consolidation Story, from Civil Rights to the Jaguars, by James B. Crooks (2004; first paperback edition, 2019)

The Seminole Wars: America's Longest Indian Conflict, by John and Mary Lou Missall (2004; first paperback edition, 2016)

The Mosquito Wars: A History of Mosquito Control in Florida, by Gordon Patterson (2004)

Seasons of Real Florida, by Jeff Klinkenberg (2004; first paperback edition, 2009)

Land of Sunshine, State of Dreams: A Social History of Modern Florida, by Gary R. Mormino (2005; first paperback edition, 2008)

Paradise Lost? The Environmental History of Florida, edited by Jack E. Davis and Raymond Arsenault (2005; first paperback edition, 2005)

Frolicking Bears, Wet Vultures, and Other Oddities: A New York City Journalist in Nineteenth-Century Florida, edited by Jerald T. Milanich (2005)

Waters Less Traveled: Exploring Florida's Big Bend Coast, by Doug Alderson (2005)

Saving South Beach, by M. Barron Stofik (2005; first paperback edition, 2012)

Losing It All to Sprawl: How Progress Ate My Cracker Landscape, by Bill Belleville (2006; first paperback edition, 2010)

Voices of the Apalachicola, compiled and edited by Faith Eidse (2006)

Floridian of His Century: The Courage of Governor LeRoy Collins, by Martin A. Dyckman (2006)

America's Fortress: A History of Fort Jefferson, Dry Tortugas, Florida, by Thomas Reid (2006; first paperback edition, 2022)

Weeki Wachee, City of Mermaids: A History of One of Florida's Oldest Roadside Attractions, by Lu Vickers (2007)

City of Intrigue, Nest of Revolution: A Documentary History of Key West in the Nineteenth Century, by Consuelo E. Stebbins (2007)

The New Deal in South Florida: Design, Policy, and Community Building, 1933–1940, edited by John A. Stuart and John F. Stack Jr. (2008)

The Enduring Seminoles: From Alligator Wrestling to Casino Gaming, Revised and Expanded Edition, by Patsy West (2008)

Pilgrim in the Land of Alligators: More Stories about Real Florida, by Jeff Klinkenberg (2008; first paperback edition, 2011)

A Most Disorderly Court: Scandal and Reform in the Florida Judiciary, by Martin A. Dyckman (2008)

A Journey into Florida Railroad History, by Gregg M. Turner (2008; first paperback edition, 2012)

Sandspurs: Notes from a Coastal Columnist, by Mark Lane (2008)

Paving Paradise: Florida's Vanishing Wetlands and the Failure of No Net Loss, by Craig Pittman and Matthew Waite (2009; first paperback edition, 2010)

Embry-Riddle at War: Aviation Training during World War II, by Stephen G. Craft (2009)

The Columbia Restaurant: Celebrating a Century of History, Culture, and Cuisine, by Andrew T. Huse, with recipes and memories from Richard Gonzmart and the Columbia restaurant family (2009)

Ditch of Dreams: The Cross Florida Barge Canal and the Struggle for Florida's Future, by Steven Noll and David Tegeder (2009; first paperback edition, 2015)

Manatee Insanity: Inside the War over Florida's Most Famous Endangered Species, by Craig Pittman (2010; first paperback edition, 2022)

Frank Lloyd Wright's Florida Southern College, by Dale Allen Gyure (2010)

Sunshine Paradise: A History of Florida Tourism, by Tracy J. Revels (2011; first paperback edition, 2020)

Hidden Seminoles: Julian Dimock's Historic Florida Photographs, by Jerald T. Milanich and Nina J. Root (2011)

Treasures of the Panhandle: A Journey through West Florida, by Brian R. Rucker (2011)

Key West on the Edge: Inventing the Conch Republic, by Robert Kerstein (2012; first paperback edition, 2022)

The Scent of Scandal: Greed, Betrayal, and the World's Most Beautiful Orchid, by Craig Pittman (2012; first paperback edition, 2014)

Backcountry Lawman: True Stories from a Florida Game Warden, by Bob H. Lee (2013; first paperback edition, 2015)

Alligators in B-Flat: Improbable Tales from the Files of Real Florida, by Jeff Klinkenberg (2013; first paperback edition, 2015)

CPSIA information can be obtained
at www.ICGtesting.com
Printed in the USA
LVHW111802230223
739999LV00003B/109